MW01234479

DISLOYAL

When the Loyal, Aren't

DISLOYAL

When the Loyal, Aren't

Paul Seger

DISLOYAL

When the Loyal, Aren't

Copyright © 2023 Paul Seger
All rights reserved.
ISBN: 9798377294184

All rights reserved solely by the author. No part of this book may be reproduced in any form without the permission of the author except in the case of brief quotations in critical articles or reviews.

Unless otherwise indicated, all Scripture quotations are from the ESV® Bible (The Holy Bible, English Standard Version®), copyright © 2001 by Crossway, a publishing ministry of Good News Publishers. Used by permission. All rights reserved.

Scripture marked KJV taken from THE KING JAMES VERSION.

Scripture marked NKJV taken from the New King James Version®. Copyright © 1982 by Thomas Nelson. Used by permission. All rights reserved.

CONTENTS

PREFACE

Some people are natural-born leaders. I am not.

The irony is that for much of my life, I've been thrust into leadership roles. This forced me to make leadership a lifelong study. This meant watching leaders carefully. It meant having mentors. It meant reading hundreds of books and articles on the topic. I've pestered leaders to figure out how they do it. I've even written a book about leadership to crystallize some of my thoughts on the topic. It has been a scramble to figure out how to do what I was supposed to do as a leader.

One topic, however, seemed to be missing in my research: the subject of disloyalty. Out of my own painful experiences, I searched for resources on the topic (Amazon lists over 60,000 books on leadership), but I found few articles or books that addressed this issue. Thus this book.

I began asking leaders if they had ever experienced disloyalty. With pain in their eyes, the overwhelming majority answered, "Yes."

To take this beyond anecdotal evidence, I launched a survey to Christian leaders and received 369 responses. Here are the questions I asked. The results are in the addendum of this book, and I regularly reference them throughout.

- ✦ I am responding to this survey as: (a ministry leader) (a business leader)

- ✦ Age: (20-29) (30-39) (40-49) (50-59) (60-69) (70+)

- ✦ Sex: (Male) (Female)

- ✦ Have you ever experienced someone being disloyal to you as a leader? (Yes) (No)

If you answer "Yes" to this question, please select one instance where this happened to you, and then continue with the following questions. If you answer "No," you can submit your survey at this time.

✦ With the one example of disloyalty you are thinking of, check as many of the boxes below that you feel would characterize the type of disloyalty you experienced.

- Public criticism of your character (lack of spiritual walk or godly characteristics)
- Public criticism of your capacity (lack of ability in an area)
- Public criticism of your position on doctrine
- Public criticism of your social/political stance
- Public criticism of your interpersonal skills (lack of empathy, care, sarcasm, cynicism, too task-oriented)
- Public criticism of your work product (speeches, events, writings)
- Gossip to undercut your credibility, challenge your position
- Outright lies or slander to destroy your reputation
- Making, participating in, organizational moves to minimize or eliminate your role
- Refusing to support you when you made organizational changes
- Refusing to support you when others challenged your role
- Other (describe)

✦ Regarding this significant disloyalty event in your life, approximately how long would you say it lasted before it was resolved? (1 day) (1 week) (1 month) (1 year) (Over a year) (It has not been resolved.)

✦ On a scale of 1-5, how severely did disloyalty impact your ministry/work? (1= low, 5 = high)

- ✦ On a scale of 1-5, how severely did disloyalty impact you personally? (1= low, 5 = high)

- ✦ On a scale of 1-5, if someone was disloyal to you, would you characterize him or her as someone who was in a close work/ministry relationship with you or a distant work/ministry relationship? (1 = close, 5 = distant)

- ✦ On a scale of 1-5, if someone was disloyal to you, would you characterize him or her as someone who was in close personal relationship with you or distant personal relationship? (1 = close, 5 = distant)

- ✦ Finally, on a related issue, have you ever been a part of an organization where unhealthy loyalty (not being allowed to question the leader, i.e., "worshipping" the leader, etc.) was practiced? (Yes, No)

The response to the survey confirmed that this is a topic worth addressing since, for most of us in leadership, it is not a question of "if" we will experience disloyalty, but "when" we will experience it. Astoundingly, 85 percent of those who responded said they had experienced disloyalty. This is not a side issue. If you haven't been stabbed in the back yet, put on your Kevlar. At the very least, undermining us as leaders distracts us from our focus. Often it derails ministry and debilitates us. It is horrific. Devastating. Soul-destroying. Agony-inducing. Disloyalty attacks the very core of our being and destroys our trust in humanity.

It is my desire that this book will help prepare us leaders for what may be inevitable and to help us walk successfully through the experience without permanently derailing or damaging the ministry.

INTRODUCTION

Though leadership books rarely address the topic of disloyalty and loyalty, wisdom literature, such as Proverbs 20:6, abounds with verses on the subject. "Many a man proclaims his own steadfast love, but a faithful man who can find?"

Characters in the Bible can also provide insight. Though there are many more examples, this book will look at ten stories in scripture: Miriam, Absalom, Satan, Peter, Judas, Ruth, Abigail, Paul, Jonathan, and Uriah. Five will be about disloyalty and five about loyalty—half negative and half positive. They will teach us how to act and how not to act.

These ten chapters have bookends. On the left side is a chapter that defines *loyalty, inordinate loyalty* and *disloyalty* and argues the case for the importance of this topic. On the right side is a summary of how we as leaders can respond to disloyalty. Our goal should be to embrace the spirit of Joseph when he said, "You meant evil against me, but God meant it for good" (Genesis 50:20). There is, however, a big gap between being offended and wholeheartedly embracing the sovereignty of God. The goal of this book is to help us do that.

1

DEFINING THE RELATIONSHIP

Benedict Arnold, Judas, Brutus, Tokyo Rose, Julius and Ethel Rosenberg, and Guy Fawkes have all become synonyms for *traitor*. Their disloyalty branded them forever.

There are often two sides to the story. Traitors are convinced that their actions are noble and warranted. For instance, Benedict Arnold spent his own money to support troops for which Congress never reimbursed him. George Washington trusted him and appointed him to command West Point. That commitment to the nation began to sour, however, when another general got the praise for a battle that Arnold had actually won. His growing realization that the current government was corrupt caused him to defect.

Regardless of motive, disloyalty brands the traitor. All the good that these people might have done was overwhelmed by one act. A life of service and loyalty was forgotten, diminished and replaced by the moniker *traitor*.

Loyalty

Loyalty is a recurring theme of scripture. There are multiple examples and theological concepts that surround the term, including *love, hesed, commitment, faithful, trust* and *covenant*, but individually these terms don't quite define the word *loyal*.

Here is a working definition of the term: Loyalty is allegiance to a person, cause, or institution through the good and the bad times.

Loyalty may refer to a commitment to a government, a sovereign, a church, a club, a country, a friend or a cause. Loyalty glues together gang members, the mafia, and pirates. Sports teams elicit extraordinary loyalty as illustrated by Chicago Cubs fans who remained enthusiastically devoted to their team despite a 108-year drought without a World Series championship.

Loyalty in sports is a powerful motivator.

Nearly 130 soccer match attendees in Malang, Indonesia, died Saturday after police sprayed tear gas in an attempt to stop fights between fans that resulted in a stampede. The incident occurred after the Indonesian Premier League's Sunday night game, when fans were upset by the loss of their team, Area Malang. Arima fans rushed to the field following the match, reports say. [1]

This is merely one story of hundreds about violent fans from opposing teams. Less volatile, but loyal, fans will spend thousands of dollars on clothing and memorabilia, plus the cost of going to games and paying $15 for a hotdog just to support their team.

Loyalty motivates family members to stick up for a criminal relative. A wife will support her mate regardless of what he has done. A brother will fight anyone who attacks his sister. Even a dog will savage someone who attacks its master.

---

[1] https://www.insider.com/deaths-hospital-fights-stampede-indonesian-soccer-match-2022-10

Great companies work hard at developing brand loyalty. In the business world you can rate your enterprise with a Net Promoter Score which measures the loyalty of your customers. The goal is to increase that loyalty because higher scores translate into higher sales and more profit. Firms like Apple can generate a cult-like following with customers willing to pay more for their product than comparable items of other brands. There is an emotional attachment that arises to religious fervor for this company. People sleep on the sidewalk to be first in line to buy the newest version of the iPhone. Some people are so committed that they tattoo the logo on their bodies.

Great leaders seek to foster loyalty to create stability in their company or organization and to provide an attractive work culture. Corporations can move forward faster because people trust each other.

The highest level of loyalty may be to a cause, but individuals are the embodiment of a cause. The scope of this book is primarily about loyalty to people, for inevitably a cause affects personal relationships.

Loyalty is a commitment to another human being. It is choosing to side with people regardless of their actions . . . not to ignore or support their actions but simply to be in their corner. It is sticking with someone through the good and the bad, the ups and the downs, winning or losing, sinfulness or holiness, thick or thin. It is constant and unqualified support for someone.

Loyalty means "I have your back." What an incredible blessing to have relationships with people who are looking out for your good. You know that they will not undermine you. They are willing to bring you unwelcome news and even correct you. They will come to you first instead of undercutting you. Loyal people don't conspire behind your back.

Deformed Loyalty

When I speak of loyalty, I am not suggesting an aberrant form I call *inordinate loyalty*. This is typically a situation where leaders do not permit followers to question or examine their actions. They refuse input or critique, demand and enforce unquestioning loyalty, and expect compliance without reservation. It is almost tantamount to worshipping the person in charge.

Cults thrive with this kind of loyalty. The leader bullies and intimidates to gain followers. Some have been known to rate followers on a loyalty scale from 1 to 10. They have spies to let them know who is not all in. I've read about leaders who say they will run over their followers if they don't fall in line. The tell-tale sign of cultic leaders is when they claim they are the only ones who are doing it right or teaching it right.

Those who comply with and submit to this kind of leadership find their identity in the leader. They protect their position and relationship with the leader by blind loyalty. They will not speak up when the actions of the leader are sinful or contradict the cause.

Dr. A. Somerville is a self-declared humanist yet has some perceptive observations about cult-like leadership. She writes:

> You are in a harmful cult or high-control group if:
> - There is opposition to critical thought,
> - And self-doubt is encouraged.
> - Magical thinking is prevalent,
> - And leaders claim to have special insight and supreme knowledge.
> - The leadership is authoritarian, charismatic and narcissistic,
> - And leaders are not accountable to other authorities.
> - There are draconian and intrusive rules for members,
> - But the leaders are above the law.
> - The flow of information is subject to censorship and control,
> - And the group as a whole is elitist, with an elite "inner circle" at its core.
> - Threats are made against members who leave,

- And outsiders or outsider groups are slandered and vilified.
- Members become increasingly isolated from former companions,
- And group identity takes precedence over (or replaces) individual identity.
- The group performs secret rites and rituals,
- And in general, their events involve mind-altering practices.
- Members frequently experience feelings of shame, guilt, fear and dread,
- And show zealous commitment, loyalty and dependence upon their leaders.
- Groups have a preoccupation with new members and proselytizing;
- They target the vulnerable with "love-bombing" and idealistic goals.
- There is evidence of economic or financial exploitation,
- And of punitive punishment, even physical abuse.
- There is evidence of sexual exploitation,
- And women, especially, are tightly controlled.
- Deception is normalized, and the ends always justify the means.[2]

The term "drinking the Kool-Aid" was coined from this kind of loyalty when Jim Jones led nine hundred people in Guyana to their death by poisoned drink. Amazingly, people continue to follow "prophets" who forecast the end of the world but keep revising their predictions when they don't come true. That is blind loyalty.

2 https://secularliturgies.wordpress.com/2020/02/24/the-25-signs-youre-in-a-high-control-group-or-cult-by-anastasia-somerville-wong/

Scripture tells us: "Put not your trust in princes, in a son of man, in whom there is no salvation. When his breath departs, he returns to the earth; on that very day his plans perish" (Psalm 146:3-4). Jeremiah 17:5 gives a curse on those who trust in man. Jesus did not commit himself to men (John 2:24-25). Leaders deserve our support, but they are fallible. Loyalty does not overlook the weaknesses or sin of a leader. Blind loyalty will eventually lead to disappointment.

In my survey, 57 percent responded that they have been part of an organization that practiced unhealthy loyalty. Inordinate loyalty is just as destructive as disloyalty. Neither one is good for the leader but for different reasons. Disloyalty destroys a relationship. Inordinate loyalty destroys the leader. It does not serve the leader well to be surrounded by those who will not confront his sinful actions.

In an article about toxic leadership, Cary Schmid says:

Even reasonable loyalty can't be demanded as much as it can be developed. If a strong team loyalty isn't growing organically, can it really be coerced into place? Reasonable loyalty grows from the context of integrity and humility. When the team is healthy in biblical direction and relationships, loyalty grows organically from the garden of close-knit hearts. Therefore, it generally doesn't need to be emphasized, as much as appreciated. A leader should be humbled that co-laborers would develop an appropriate sense of support and commitment, not only to the leader, but to the whole team and to the cause of the gospel.[3]

The Apostle Peter makes this clear:

So I exhort the elders among you, as a fellow elder and a witness of the sufferings of Christ, as well as a partaker in the glory that is going to be revealed: shepherd the flock of God that is among you, exercising oversight, not under com-

---

3 https://caryschmidt.com/2016/07/14-qualities-of-toxic-leadership/

pulsion, but willingly, as God would have you; not for shameful gain, but eagerly; **not domineering over those in your charge**, but being examples to the flock. (1 Peter 5:1-3, Emphasis added)

This echoes the words of Jesus when he said:

You know that the rulers of the Gentiles lord it over them, and their great ones exercise authority over them. **It shall not be so among you**. But whoever would be great among you must be your servant, and whoever would be first among you must be your slave. (Matthew 20:25-27, Emphasis added)

Pastors may be tempted to justify their actions by Hebrews 13:17:

Obey your leaders and submit to them, for they are keeping watch over your souls, as those who will have to give an account. Let them do this with joy and not with groaning, for that would be of no advantage to you.

Isolating this verse as a proof text neglects other passages like 2 Corinthians 1:24 where Paul said, "Not that we lord it over your faith, but we work with you for your joy, for you stand firm in your faith." This apostle had authority none of us possess, but he still restrained his demands for loyalty. He went so far as to say, "But even if we or an angel from heaven should preach to you a gospel contrary to the one we preached to you, let him be accursed" (Galatians 1:8). Obviously, there are limits to our loyalty.

Perhaps this mindset comes from confusing the difference between the church and Israel. We look at strong leaders like Moses, Joshua, David or Solomon and take their leadership style as a model. In Old Testament times, the leaders of Israel were both spiritual and political leaders of a kingdom or theocracy. The church is entirely different. Pastors are not meant to be autocratic generals or potentates. As shepherds, their authority extends only as far as scripture.

Loyalty includes confrontation. Disloyal people may choose to go behind the back of the leader instead of confronting him, but autocratic leaders do not allow confrontation. Insecure leaders do not allow followers to question their decisions. Love, however, demands that we speak into the lives of others and point out where they may have the wrong trajectory. It is not serving a leader well to let him recklessly career down a hill of self-destruction, and it is dangerous to follow a leader who does not have accountability. Any leader who requires unquestioning obedience is suspect. These self-appointed leaders prey on weak people to build their empire.

Proverbs 27:6 says, "Faithful are the wounds of a friend." A loyal acquaintance is willing to confront. It may be painful and stressful, but a devoted friend wants what is best, and that sometimes means the leader needs a course correction. That kind of confrontation has at least two characteristics. First, it must be done with humility and with grace. Second, it ought to take place privately, one-on-one.

The military thrives on loyalty and obedience. The chain of command will only work if soldiers do what they are told. They are trained to follow commands even if it means rushing forward to their death. But even the military recognizes the need to temper that loyalty with other factors. Officers are expected to disobey a command if it violates certain criteria. Here are some illustrations of when disobedience is condoned:

- If the officer cannot live with obeying the order, then he must disobey and accept the consequences.
- When I cannot look at myself in the mirror afterwards.
- When I deem the order to be immoral.
- When it is going to lead to mission failure.
- When it will get someone injured or killed needlessly.
- When it will cause military or institutional disaster.[4]

---

4 https://www.army.mil/article/47175/breaking_ranks_dissent_and_the_military_professional

This article goes on to say: "These comments reflect the view that the military professional has moral obligations more fundamental than obedience and loyalty to their leaders, civilian or military."[5] Our first commitment is to Christ and His cause. We don't get a pass for sinful behavior because our leader told us to do something contrary to scripture. Loyalty has its limits.

In an article titled "When can a soldier disobey an order," John Ford tells this story:

In March 1968, a U.S. infantry platoon under the command of 2nd Lt. William "Rusty" Calley conducted a raid of a hamlet called My Lai in Quang Ngai Province of South Vietnam. After taking the hamlet, Calley ordered his men to round up the remaining civilians, herd them into a ditch, and gun them down. Somewhere between 350 and 500 civilians were killed on Calley's instruction.

Calley was court-martialed for his actions and charged with 22 counts of murder. At his trial, he testified that his company commander, Capt. Ernest Medina, had ordered him to kill "every living thing" in My Lai, telling him there were no civilians there, only Viet Cong. When Calley radioed back to Medina that the platoon had rounded up a large number of unarmed civilians, he claimed Medina told him to "waste them." Essentially, Calley defended gunning down hundreds of civilians by saying he was just following orders from his superiors (It should be noted that Medina denied giving these orders).

But Calley was unable to hide behind this defense. Every military officer swears an oath upon commissioning. That oath is not to obey all orders. It is to "preserve, protect, and defend the Constitution of the United States against all enemies, foreign and domestic." It is simply wrong to say Calley had an obligation to follow any order no matter what. His first obliga-

5 https://www.army.mil/article/47175/breaking_ranks_dissent_and_the_military_professional

tion was to obey the law, and the law prohibits the deliberate killing of unarmed civilians.[6]

The Apostle Paul said, "Be imitators of me, as I am of Christ" (1 Corinthians 11:1). It may seem arrogant and self-serving for Paul to command his followers to fall in line, but the rest of the verse says, "Even as I also am of Christ." The caveat for following leaders is that they are following Jesus. If their actions or commands are not Christlike, then the believer should not blindly fulfill their wishes.

God unreservedly loves us and is loyal to His people, but that does not mean He overlooks or keeps silent about sin and injustice. God holds people accountable.

Disloyalty

Sometimes it is easier to understand a term by its antonym. Scripture may refer to disloyalty as *treachery*. Various translations render the Hebrew word as *disloyal, traitor,* or *betray*. Or we might use the terms *unfaithful, undependable, unreliable,* or *untrustworthy*. A core concept of disloyalty is intent to harm someone. In popular terms we might say that disloyalty is when we feel stabbed in the back.

Bob Sorge puts it this way:

> To be disloyal is to turn away from a relationship of mutual trust and do harm to the other. The harm can take the form of criticism, slander, backbiting, reproach, false witness, undermining, robbery, defamation, dishonor, personal attack, or something similar. Disloyalty is not simply an absence of loyalty. Disloyalty steps beyond neutrality and somehow hurts the one with whom it was once aligned.[7]

Disloyalty is a powerful motivator with disastrous results. It will shatter relationships. Commitment to a political party can

---

6 https://warontherocks.com/2017/07/when-can-a-soldier-disobey-an-order/

7 Bob Sorge, *Loyalty: The Reach of the Noble Heart,* Oasis House, 2004, p. 146.

separate friendships. A citizen will risk imprisonment and possible death for being a traitor. An employee will risk job security and paycheck to share information with a competitor. Disloyalty may cause irrational behavior.

The business world continually wrestles with disloyalty. A couple generations ago, people would work for one company their entire life. They would put in their 45 years and retire with a pension provided by that corporation. That was considered company loyalty. But that is no longer the case. According to one study, companies lose, on average, half of their employees every four years. Loyalty is to self. People view themselves as independent contractors, and each job is a steppingstone to enhance their resume. The result is that people commonly work for a dozen or more companies in a lifetime.

In my survey taken for this book, 85 percent of Christian leaders said they walked through this valley. Many biographies of great Christian leaders include their dark days of disloyalty. Considered America's first great theologian, Jonathan Edwards was a leading voice in the Great Awakening. As a speaker and author he stirred the early colonies to repentance and revival, yet someone in his church led a campaign to fire him, leaving him unemployed and caring for a family of ten children. As someone has said, "If you enter the boxing ring, be ready for some body blows."

Unfortunately, disloyalty is something most pastors will experience. It is incongruous, but a church can be a brutal environment. In a podcast, John MacArthur related an experience early in his pastorate that he labeled "Black Tuesday."

MacArthur: So I was in the office, and there were five guys there, and I said, "I'm so glad you guys are my friends. So thankful for you." And one of them immediately said, "If you think we are your friends, you have another think coming." I'll never forget that line. I was just stunned. Really. Yeah, those were guys I had personally discipled. Young guys around my age. One of them had basically sown the seeds consistently of hostility toward me.

Host: Not only had several turned against MacArthur, but they also sought out others to convince them that the pastor was up to no good.

MacArthur: It was full blown, as the French say, a *coup d'état*. They went to the elders and said, "You have to get John out of the pulpit; he's too powerful. Too much influence." There was one of them, a brand-new guy, who was doing an internship there, and he joined them and was living in my house with his wife. And I went to him one day when he came home and told him I knew what he was doing. "You are a guest in my house, living in my house, and you are doing everything you can to join a conspiracy to undermine me?"

Host: Why were these men so hostile? Why did they turn against him?

MacArthur: It is always jealousy. It rose out of the envy of someone who was close. There is a sort of pathology to it. There were young guys who would come, and I was kind of the hero for a while, then I became sort of a problem to them because of envy or jealousy. Then I went from being a hero to being an anti-hero. And that shift in their need to elevate themselves they felt they needed to undermine me. And it only takes one person to do that.[8]

Loyalty and disloyalty are major themes in scripture, and we have multiple stories of both. This book will deal with ten of them. They are theological constructs that guide our relationships with each other and with God. For example, 1 Kings 8:61 says, "Let your heart therefore be wholly true to the LORD our God, walking in his statutes and keeping his commandments, as at this day." In the New Testament there are multiple references to faithfulness to God as a baseline commitment to Him. Then there are

---

8 https://macarthurcenter.org/the-expositor/Podcast Episode 8: Faithful, October 28, 2021

instructions to servants (employees) that they need to show "all good faith, so that in everything they may adorn the doctrine of God our Savior" (Titus 2:10).

God is seeking loyalty in us. "For the eyes of the LORD run to and fro throughout the whole earth, to give strong support to those whose heart is blameless toward him. You have done foolishly in this, for from now on you will have wars" (2 Chronicles 16:9). It is my hope that this book will further entrench loyalty in your heart and actions and that God will find in you a heart that is loyal to Him. I end this chapter with a loyalty story from baseball.

As a devoted Boston Red Sox fan, it pains me to admit that Babe Ruth was one of the greatest baseball players in the history of the game. His bat had the power of a cannon, and his record of 714 home runs remained unbroken until Hank Aaron came along. The Babe was the idol of sports fans everywhere, but in time age took its toll, and his popularity began to wane.

As his illustrious career was winding down, the Yankees eventually traded him to the Braves. In one of his last games, Babe Ruth began to falter. He struck out multiple times and made several errors that allowed the Cincinnati Reds to score five runs in one inning. As the Babe walked toward the dugout, chin down and dejected, there rose from the stands an enormous storm of boos and catcalls. Some fans even shook their fists at him.

Then something wonderful happened. A little boy jumped over the railing, and with tears streaming down his cheeks he ran out to the great athlete. Unashamedly, he flung his arms around the Babe's legs and held on tightly. Ruth scooped him up, hugged him, and set him down again. Patting him gently on the head, they joined hands and walked off the field together.

That little boy taught a whole stadium of baseball fans a lesson in loyalty. Loyalty means faithfulness and devotion to something or someone, even when it is difficult. When your favorite sports team doesn't make the playoffs or your favorite athlete falls into a slump, it would be easier to root for someone else. Likewise, loyalty to anything from automobiles to laundry detergents is difficult when you can get a better deal on something else. Loyalty is hard—that is why it is so hard to come by.[9]

---

9 https://www.franklinunitedchurch.com/2013/09/15/loyalty-to-the-gospel2-timothy-18-14/

2

MIRIAM

A classic study in disloyalty

Scripture narratives teach us how to live. "Now these things happened to them as an example, but they were written down for our instruction, on whom the end of the ages has come" (1 Corinthians 10:11). Thus it is appropriate that we delve into the stories of loyalty and disloyalty to understand the lessons they offer.

The story of Miriam provides an opening salvo on the topic of disloyalty. I will introduce here a list of basic issues that surround most instances of disloyalty, but you will see a recurring theme in the other stories. Common denominators seem to surface whenever there is a breach in relationships. This chapter will serve to identify them, and later chapters will dig deeper into the topics.

Verbalizing Discontent

The story begins with these words: "Miriam and Aaron spoke against Moses" (Numbers 12:1).

Disloyalty is not about thinking negative things; it is about speaking them. While there may be instances when we wonder about the direction of a leader, disloyalty is about verbalizing our thoughts. It is not disloyal to be analytical and discerning, but it is when we talk openly to others with intentions to harm.

James 3 speaks directly to this issue. "If anyone does not stumble in what he says, he is a perfect man, able also to bridle his whole body" (2). We can move into sin because of what we say, but James takes it one step further. He says we are perfect if we never get ourselves into trouble with our tongue. It is verbalizing our thoughts that creates the problems of disloyalty. This principle may seem overly simplistic, but it is critical to our understanding. We become disloyal when we start talking about someone behind his or her back.

James goes on to say,

How great a forest is set ablaze by such a small fire! And the tongue is a fire, a world of unrighteousness. The tongue is set among our members, staining the whole body, setting on fire the entire course of life, and set on fire by hell. (3:5-6)

James warns us to be careful about what we say because verbalizing our discontent or disagreements is such a destructive force. Disloyalty can burn down a whole jungle.

Loyalty demands that we talk to the individual with whom we disagree. Disloyalty includes undermining others by talking about them. Anytime we hear people talking negatively about another person, we should ask if they have already talked to that individual about the issue they are raising (Matthew 18:15). If they have not done that, you are probably observing disloyalty in its seed form.

Betraying Close Relationships

While it is possible to be disloyal to a cause, this book primarily discusses loyalty to individuals. My survey indicated that 68 percent of the responders experienced disloyalty from close or very close co-workers. Disloyalty from any source can be egregious, but it is particularly painful if it comes through someone we know.

Of all people, you would think a sibling would stick up for you. Moses' sister Miriam pulled him from the bulrushes and saved his life as a baby. As his sister, I'm sure she kept track of his experiences as he grew up in the palace. Moses' brother Aaron was also extremely close. God chose him to be Moses' sidekick and literally to be his voice (Exodus 4:10-16). It was probably Aaron who did the speaking when they confronted Pharaoh (Exodus 7:1). Miriam and Aaron were there when Moses led the nation of Israel through the Red Sea and into the desert. They were by his side when the nation rebelled. They stood with him as they saw God provide manna and water. This triad should have been inseparable . . . but they were not.

This is what makes disloyalty so painful. It is often a friend or even a relative who stabs us in the back. It seems incongruous that friends would turn against us, but we shouldn't be surprised. Psalm 41:9 warns us of this when it forecasted the betrayal of Jesus by Judas. "Even my close friend in whom I trusted, who ate my bread, has lifted his heel against me." It happened to David through Absalom, Paul through Demas, and Jesus through Peter. The closer the relationship, the more devastating the experience. David wrote this heart-wrenching statement:

For it is not an enemy who taunts me—then I could bear it; it is not an adversary who deals insolently with me—then I could hide from him. But it is you, a man, my equal, my companion, my familiar friend. We used to take sweet counsel together; within God's house we walked in the throng. (Psalm 55:12-14)

One of the most famous assassinations in history was Julius Caesar on the Ides of March, 44 BC. Marcus Julius Brutus led the insurrection of sixty other senators because they believed that Caesar's dictatorship was undermining the Roman Republic. On that fateful day, Brutus led the senators in stabbing him twenty-three times. There is some debate about whether Brutus was the illegitimate son of Julius Caesar, but true or not, Brutus was part of the inner circle of leadership in Rome and closely associated with Caesar. Thus Shakespeare includes the phrase *Et tu, Brute?* (You too, Brutus?), though it may have been spoken in Greek *(Kai su, teknon?)* or perhaps not at all. Whichever utterance it was, Shakespeare captured the idea that it was a friend who had led in the treason. Though there is debate over the historicity of this story, it illustrates the principle that disloyalty comes from an existing relationship.

Destroying Unity

Miriam and Aaron were part of the leadership team for the nation of Israel. Aaron was the high priest and mouthpiece for Moses. Miriam was a prophetess who led in worship (Exodus 15:20). We even have the words of a song she wrote as the nation celebrated their exodus from Egypt and escape from the Egyptians (Exodus 15:21).

It might be palatable to accept that followers in the crowd would be disloyal, but it upends our logic to think that co-workers and fellow leaders would turn against us. Yet many of us know stories of a youth pastor who undermined the pastor and led a group down the street to start a new church. We should not be surprised when it is a deacon, elder, or fellow pastor who leads a revolt.

There has only been one time in five decades of ministry when I considered quitting. It was because of disloyalty. An elder in our church disrupted the unity and undermined the direction and leadership of the rest of the team. It was unexpected. It was devastating. It caused emotional agony and loss of sleep. It diverted my attention from the main focus of my work. It was so traumatic that it caused me to consider abandoning my calling.

In his book *Antagonist in the Church,* Kenneth C. Haugk writes about a common problem in many churches where a leader disrupts the unity by disloyalty. The irony is that this person is by all outward appearances a committed and dedicated worker in the church. This person is often the first there when the doors open and the last to leave. He seems to be all in. From all appearances, he is loyal. Then out of nowhere, he unsheathes his sword and attacks the leadership.

Our reaction might be to question how we could have ever trusted these leaders. We were working shoulder to shoulder and walking through some valleys together. These were our comrades in arms. These are people who were seemingly united with us in the mission and vision. We dreamed and worked together on the future of the ministry. It seemed we were pulling together in the same direction—and then out of nowhere: disloyalty. It stings.

One of the ironies of disloyalty is that it undermines people's trust in the disloyal person. Often the motive for disloyalty is to gather a following, but in the end it backfires, because people innately know they can't trust disloyal people. Isaiah warned against this.

> Ah, you destroyer, who yourself have not been destroyed, you traitor, whom none has betrayed! When you have ceased to destroy, you will be destroyed; and when you have finished betraying, they will betray you. (Isaiah 33:1)

Don't be surprised if a Miriam or an Aaron arises from your leadership team.

Misdirecting

Miriam and Aaron claimed their problem with Moses was a matter of authority: "Has the LORD indeed spoken only through

19

Moses? Has he not spoken through us also?" (Numbers 12:2). But that wasn't the real problem. It was a smokescreen for their ulterior motives. The issue driving their disloyalty was an interpersonal one: "Miriam and Aaron spoke against Moses because of the Cushite woman whom he had married, for he had married a Cushite woman" (Numbers 12:1).

Often the disloyal person will not own up to his or her real agenda. It is a little uncertain about the identity of "Cush," but it was probably a country in Africa, implying Moses' wife had a darker skin color. Perhaps it was racism that inflamed Miriam and Aaron. Perhaps they were upset because Moses had not married within the nation of Israel, and they had a legitimate concern about her religion.

An alternative reason could be a case of sibling rivalry. Or maybe they were upset over their loss of influence and control. Up until this time, older sister Miriam had major influence on Moses' decisions, but Moses' new wife probably took Miriam's place as the leading lady of the team.

"The heart is deceitful," says Jeremiah 17:9. Because we can so easily be self-deceived, we also deceive others. The real agenda for our actions is often disguised. Jesus put it this way:

> For from within, out of the heart of man, come evil thoughts, sexual immorality, theft, murder, adultery, coveting, wickedness, deceit, sensuality, envy, slander, pride, foolishness. All these evil things come from within, and they defile a person. (Mark 7:21-22)

Regardless of the reason for their rebellion, they were not being forthright about their real agenda.

Undermining Authority

Disloyalty is often a power struggle because authority is intrinsic to leadership. Leaders have the authority to make decisions and to lead, so to dethrone a leader, you have to take away or diminish their authority. That is exactly what Miriam and Aaron tried.

Disloyalty manifests itself in a variety of ways. The 369 leaders in my survey cited the following types of attacks to their leadership:

11% Public criticism of your capacity (lack of ability in an area)

16% Gossip to undercut your position or challenge your position

12% Outright lies or slander to destroy your reputation

10% Making, participating in, organizational moves to minimize or eliminate your role

10% Refusing to support you when you made organizational changes

8% Refusing to support you when others challenged your role

All these actions undermine the authority of a leader. This concept goes way back to the fall of Satan. It was his ambition to become like God, to have the prestige and authority of the Creator. When the Devil brought sin into the world, he went straight for the jugular and questioned the authority of God. "He said to the woman, 'Did God actually say, "You shall not eat of any tree in the garden"?'" (Genesis 3:1).

The irony is that Moses was not power hungry. "Now the man Moses was very meek, more than all people who were on the face of the earth" (Numbers 12:3). He never wanted the job in the first place. While some leaders are indeed driven by power, there are many who are thrust into leadership against their natural desires. Men like Gideon had to be talked into leadership.

God came to Moses' defense:

And he said, "Hear my words: If there is a prophet among you, I the LORD make myself known to him in a vision; I speak with him in a dream. Not so with my servant Moses. He is faithful in all my house. With him I speak mouth to mouth, clearly, and not in riddles, and he beholds the form of the LORD.

Why then were you not afraid to speak against my servant Moses?" (Numbers 12:6-8)

There is God-given authority in leadership, and He views it a sinful thing to attack that authority.

Disloyalty is an action that brings God to rage: "And the anger of the LORD was kindled against them, and he departed" (Numbers 12:9). It is a dangerous thing to attack authority that God has installed. That is why scripture says: "Do not admit a charge against an elder except on the evidence of two or three witnesses" (1 Timothy 5:19). Additionally, when scripture speaks of government, it uses words like *respect, honor, obey, submit,* and *be subject to.* Disloyalty undermines authority.

Recruiting Others

Disloyal people are not satisfied being alone in an insurrection. They obviously feel something is serious enough that other people need to get involved as well. Revolts don't go very well if there is only one person. Church splits happen because multiple people were recruited; otherwise it would just be one individual leaving the church.

It isn't clear whether Aaron recruited Miriam or the other way around, but one thing is certain: there were two of them. One of them initiated the first conversation. Aaron was certainly recruitable. He had been disloyal to Moses in the past. While Moses was on the mountain receiving the Ten Commandments, the people got impatient and approached Aaron asking him to take charge and create other gods. Aaron led the initiative to create a golden calf and start a new religion for Israel (Exodus 32). Perhaps Miriam saw him as vulnerable and already had a bent toward disloyalty and thus got him on board.

Disloyal people will often say, "There are others who agree with me" or "Others are saying. . . ." Cowardly people don't want to stand on their own. They need others to give them fortitude and credibility. This happened with Absalom when he "stole the hearts of the men of Israel" (2 Samuel 15:6) to lead an insurrection against David. The essence of disloyalty is going behind someone's back, so it is only logical that they want others to join them.

Labeling Disloyalty

Aaron recognized his disloyalty as sin. "And Aaron said to Moses, 'Oh, my lord, do not punish us because we have done foolishly and have sinned'" (Numbers 12:11). Aaron knew immediately that his actions were displeasing to God. Many sins can be tied up in the bundle of disloyalty such as jealousy, coveting, racism, hatred, and gossip.

Properly labeling disloyalty as sin helps us know what to do: confess it and abandon it. It is something for which we can receive forgiveness and have relationships restored. Defining disloyalty as sin makes it easier to resolve. There is no ambiguity about the topic. It is just wrong.

The Impact of Disloyalty

The sin of disloyalty is not private. Miriam experienced the immediate discipline of God by contracting leprosy, but the impact of her actions affected other people as well. It slowed down forward progress for the entire nation. Scripture says that "Miriam was shut outside the camp seven days, and the people did not set out on the march till Miriam was brought in again" (Numbers 12:15).

Disloyalty wastes time and energy. Handling the issue distracts a leader from his main task. It diverts everyone's attention and makes it hard to concentrate on forward movement. It may absorb the leader's attention for weeks and months, and sometimes he may never quite recover. Additionally, it makes it hard for the leader to trust others, and cynicism can begin to harden sensitivity to others.

Disloyalty may have forever sidelined Miriam from leadership and ministry because this is the last time we hear anything about her until Numbers 20:1 when she dies and is buried in Kadesh. Disloyalty is like a tornado leaving a path of destruction. Know that if it happens to you, there will be others who will feel the impact.

The Leader's Response

Moses models for us a godly response when attacked. First, he asked for God's mercy on those who were disloyal. "And Moses cried to the LORD, 'O God, please heal her—please'" (Numbers 12:13). What an amazing response! Our natural proclivity is to retaliate or at least rejoice that our betrayer got what she deserved. But a godly leader understands human frailty and wants the best for everyone.

Second, Moses let God take care of the problem. Instead of defending himself, Moses stood back and watched God in action.

And suddenly the LORD said to Moses and to Aaron and Miriam, "Come out, you three, to the tent of meeting." And the three of them came out. And the LORD came down in a pillar of cloud and stood at the entrance of the tent and called Aaron and Miriam, and they both came forward. And he said, "Hear my words: If there is a prophet among you, I the LORD make myself known to him in a vision; I speak with him in a dream. Not so with my servant Moses. He is faithful in all my house. With him I speak mouth to mouth, clearly, and not in riddles, and he beholds the form of the LORD. Why then were you not afraid to speak against my servant Moses?" And the anger of the LORD was kindled against them, and he departed. (Numbers 12:4-9)

Here is what scripture says about retaliation:

Repay no one evil for evil, but give thought to do what is honorable in the sight of all. If possible, so far as it depends on you, live peaceably with all. Beloved, never avenge yourselves, but leave it to the wrath of God, for it is written, "Vengeance is mine, I will repay, says the LORD." To the contrary, "if your enemy is hungry, feed him; if he is thirsty, give him something to drink; for by so doing you will heap burning coals on his head." Do not be overcome by evil, but overcome evil with good. (Romans 12:17-21)

Leaving retribution to God is a challenging thing to do. Time, however, will vindicate us. Moses continued in his role while Miriam faded into the background.

3

ABSALOM

Who is the guilty party?

The story of Absalom and his father David is painful. His betrayal fits all the classic characteristics that are in the story of Miriam and Moses, but this instance has an additional key lesson to learn about disloyalty: there are two sides to a story and probably no innocent parties. Before we look at that, however, it is important to understand the background to the story.

Absalom was the third son of King David. He was physically attractive.

Now in all Israel there was no one so much to be praised for his handsome appearance as Absalom. From the sole of his foot to the crown of his head there was no blemish in him. (2 Samuel 14:25)

His hair was so thick that, once a year when he cut it, his locks weighed five pounds. It seemed that everyone loved him.

In addition to his good looks, he undoubtedly had some natural charisma that helped draw people to him.

We read about his treason in 2 Samuel 15:3-6 when he "stole the hearts of the men of Israel." He eventually declared himself king in a full-blown insurrection. But what led to this?

The story goes back five years to when David's first son forced himself on his half-sister. Tamar was beautiful and became the object of Amnon's lust to the point that he raped her. Absalom learned about it and took Tamar into his home to provide refuge for her. David also learned of the situation but did nothing about it. Daily, for two years, Absalom remembered the injustice to his sister, while waiting for his father to do something. Eventually, Absalom took matters into his own hands. He invited Amnon to a party where he had his servants kill him.

Absalom fled to another country to live near his grandfather, the king of Geshur. For three years he lived in exile until Joab, commander of David's army, stepped forward to motivate Absalom's return. David agreed with the proviso that he stay in his own home and not see him. For two years, Absalom lived in exile in his own home in Jerusalem but finally called an end to the arrangement by approaching Joab.

Absalom answered Joab, "Behold, I sent word to you, 'Come here, that I may send you to the king, to ask, "Why have I come from Geshur? It would be better for me to be there still." Now therefore let me go into the presence of the king, and if there is guilt in me, let him put me to death.'" (2 Samuel 14:32)

Joab then arranged for Absalom to appear before David, but reconciliation still did not take place. Absalom moved forward with a plan to topple his father from the throne. The story goes on like this:

After this Absalom got himself a chariot and horses, and fifty men to run before him. And Absalom used to rise early and stand beside the way of the gate . . . Then Absalom would say, "Oh that I were judge in the land! Then every man with a dispute or cause might come to me, and I would give him justice." And whenever a man came near to pay homage to him, he would put out his hand and take hold of him and kiss him. Thus Absalom did to all of Israel who came to the king for judgment. So Absalom stole the hearts of the men of Israel. (2 Samuel 15:1–6)

The story doesn't end there. The seeds of disloyalty germinated to the point of a full-blown insurrection when Absalom "sent secret messengers throughout all the tribes of Israel, saying, 'As soon as you hear the sound of the trumpet, then say, "Absalom is king at Hebron!"'" (2 Samuel 15:10).

The coup was reported to David: "The hearts of the men of Israel have gone after Absalom" (2 Samuel 15:13). This rebellion rallied troops faithful to David to mount a war against Absalom who had gained a following of at least 12,000 men by this time (2 Samuel 17:1). Absalom had wrested the allegiance of the elders of Israel away from his father to support him instead (2 Samuel 17:4). A battle ensued in the forest of Ephraim with the result of 20,000 men losing their lives. As Absalom was escaping on the back of a donkey, he rode under a tree where his hair caught in the branches, leaving him hanging until Joab found him and killed him.

Blaming the Right Person

It would be logical to lay all the blame on Absalom for this tragic story, but David had a part to play in this too. This does not relieve Absalom of any guilt, but the catalyst for the disloyalty began when David failed to deal with the sin of Amnon. Even though David knew about the rape, he did nothing to bring justice to the situation. As the king and as a political leader, one of his main responsibilities was to execute justice for the nation, and he failed in one of his most basic duties.

This failure marinated in the soul of Absalom for two years as he cared for his sister Tamar. David's lack of action turned from smoldering resentment to treason and triggered this entire episode. David must bear some responsibility for Absalom's actions.

A leader will commonly dismiss disloyalty as "their sin." But part of the problem could lie at the feet of the leader, the one who was betrayed. Just because someone is disloyal doesn't mean the other person is innocent.

As previously mentioned, Benedict Arnold is synonymous with treason, but there is a backstory. His commitment to the Continental Army was unquestionable, and victories were epic, especially his valor at the Battle of Saratoga in 1777 where he was shot in the leg and limped the rest of his life. Although he was a loyal and heroic general, politics, cronyism, petty jealousy, and insider dealing sidelined Benedict. As he learned more about the corruption in government, the more disenchanted he became. This new government that was forming was just as bad as the British government they were seeking to separate from. He eventually turned his allegiance back to the British. Some historians have wondered whether Benedict Arnold betrayed his country or whether his country betrayed him.

One of our first reactions when someone has been disloyal should be to stop and evaluate what we might have done to contribute to this. Frustration over our leadership or other failures may have caused disloyalty. We should never presume our own innocence. Disloyalty is rarely a one-sided issue.

Three basic principles flow from this concept.

1. All leaders are sinners and thus fallible, and their actions or inaction may be the reason for disloyalty. Perhaps one of the reasons for David's lack of action was his lingering guilt over his sin with Bathsheba. He couldn't bring himself to mete out justice on someone else when he was guilty of the same sin. But even if that is not the case, and even though he was a man after God's own heart, David was a still a sinner. It is rather brash for any leader to assume he is the innocent party. There are always two sides to the story.

2. I don't know who first coined this statement, so I don't know who to credit, but it has been around as long as I can remember: "Within every criticism, there is a kernel of truth." We may receive disapproval, and 95 percent of it could be unfounded, but there might be 5 percent that is true. The role of the leader is to accept responsibility for his 5 percent.

3. I also don't know who should get credit for this statement: "The first responsibility of leadership is to define reality." The integrity of a leader is built on his ability to see things as they really are. It is not possible to fix something if one does not view it as broken. Perhaps David was in denial about the situation. As leaders, we should assume we have a blind side. There could just be something negative about us that we don't see clearly. We need the objectivity of a friend or neutral party to point out our faults.

Ignoring the Real Problem

At the heart of disloyalty is some form of conflict which should be seen as inevitable. We can either leverage the conflict for growth or ignore it until it erupts. David chose the latter. The problem with ignoring the clash is that it doesn't go away by itself. It festers until it metastasizes into a colossal problem.

Thus organizations like Peacemakers provide training in handling conflict. Equipping and preparing people for conflict is a crucial step in averting disloyalty. According to my survey, most of the time there was no resolution to the disloyalty. Perhaps it is because we have not been adequately trained in handling conflict. It is not a matter of "if" but rather "when" conflict will take place, so we might as well get ready for it.

Ignoring disloyalty gains nothing. We must be proactive in seeking resolution even if the chances of success are slim. Despite that, we are instructed: "If your brother sins against you, go and tell him his fault, between you and him alone. If he listens to you, you have gained your brother" (Matthew 18:5).

There is a positive side to being betrayed: it advances our sanctification. Thus, the person turning against us is actually serving us as we are forced to finetune our walk with God. Interpersonal conflict is an opportunity to learn and grow. We discover more about grace, forgiveness, humility, listening, confession, repentance, kindness, love, reconciliation, and of course, the gospel. Jesus put it this way: "Blessed are the peacemakers, for they shall be called sons of God" (Matthew 5:9). The Apostle Paul said this: "Bearing with one another and, if one has a complaint against another, forgiving each other; as the LORD has forgiven you, so you also must forgive" (Colossians 3:13).

Joseph took the high road when he said to his betraying brothers, "As for you, you meant evil against me, but God meant it for good" (Genesis 50:20). We would not blame Joseph for holding a grudge, but he saw the good in his experience and chose to focus on that. That should be the spirit of the betrayed: look for the good in bad things that happen to us.

In addition to the concept that leaders sometimes contribute to disloyalty, Absalom's story checks many of the boxes that characterized Miriam's experience. Without commenting further, notice the scriptures that underscore the ingredients of disloyalty.

Verbalizing Discontent

Then Absalom would say, "Oh that I were judge in the land! Then every man with a dispute or cause might come to me, and I would give him justice." (2 Samuel 15:4)

Betraying Close Relationships

Now, Absalom, David's son . . . (2 Samuel 13:1)

Destroying Unity

After this Absalom got himself a chariot and horses, and fifty men to run before him. (2 Samuel 15:1)

Misdirecting

And at the end of four years Absalom said to the king, "Please let me go and pay my vow, which I have vowed to the LORD, in Hebron. For your servant vowed a vow while I lived at Geshur in Aram, saying, 'If the LORD will indeed bring me back to Jerusalem, then I will offer worship to the LORD.'" The king said to him, "Go in peace." So he arose and went to Hebron. But Absalom sent secret messengers throughout all the tribes of Israel, saying, "As soon as you hear the sound of the trumpet, then say, 'Absalom is king at Hebron!'" With Absalom went two hundred men from Jerusalem who were invited guests, and they went in their innocence and knew nothing. And while Absalom was offering the sacrifices, he sent for Ahithophel the Gilonite, David's counselor, from his city Giloh. And the conspiracy grew strong, and the people with Absalom kept increasing. (2 Samuel 15:7-12)

Undermining Authority

And Absalom used to rise early and stand beside the way of the gate. And when any man had a dispute to come before the king for judgment, Absalom would call to him and say, "From what city are you?" And when he said, "Your servant is of such and such a tribe in Israel," Absalom would say to him, "See, your claims are good and right, but there is no man designated by the king to hear you." Then Absalom would say, "Oh that I were judge in the land! Then every man with a dispute or cause might come to me, and I would give him justice." And whenever a man came near to pay homage to him, he would put out his hand and take hold of him and kiss him. Thus Absalom did to all of Israel who came to the king for judgment. So Absalom stole the hearts of the men of Israel. (2 Samuel 15:2-6)

Recruiting Others

And the conspiracy grew strong, and the people with Absalom kept increasing. (2 Samuel 15:12)

And when Hushai the Archite, David's friend, came to Absalom, Hushai said to Absalom, "Long live the king! Long live the king!" And Absalom said to Hushai, "Is this your loyalty to your friend? Why did you not go with your friend?" And Hushai said to Absalom, "No, for whom the LORD and this people and all the men of Israel have chosen, his I will be, and with him I will remain. And again, whom should I serve? Should it not be his son? As I have served your father, so I will serve you." (2 Samuel 16:16-19)

Ahithophel was a counsellor for David, but he also got caught up in the betrayal and sided with Absalom with disastrous results.

The Impact of Disloyalty

Disloyalty causes excruciating pain. When Absalom had Amnon killed, he went into exile across the Jordan. Not only was he forced away from home, friends, and family, but we read that David mourned many days for his son (2 Samuel 13:37). This, however, was not limited to this one family; it affected David's army and eventually the entire nation.

It was told Joab, "Behold, the king is weeping and mourning for Absalom." So the victory that day was turned into mourning for all the people, for the people heard that day, "The king is grieving for his son." And the people stole into the city that day as people steal in who are ashamed when they flee in

34

battle. The king covered his face, and the king cried with a loud voice, "O my son Absalom, O Absalom, my son, my son!" Then Joab came into the house to the king and said, "You have today covered with shame the faces of all your servants, who have this day saved your life and the lives of your sons and your daughters and the lives of your wives and your concubines, because you love those who hate you and hate those who love you. For you have made it clear today that commanders and servants are nothing to you, for today I know that if Absalom were alive and all of us were dead today, then you would be pleased. Now therefore arise, go out and speak kindly to your servants, for I swear by the LORD, if you do not go, not a man will stay with you this night, and this will be worse for you than all the evil that has come upon you from your youth until now." Then the king arose and took his seat in the gate. And the people were all told, "Behold, the king is sitting in the gate." And all the people came before the king. Now Israel had fled every man to his own home. (2 Samuel 19:1-8)

Disloyalty impacts more than just two people. The footprint of a relationship explosion can be massive. At the very least it will affect co-workers or family members, but it could impact a church, an organization, or an entire nation.

The Leader's Response

The insurrection was in full motion: it meant war. Despite all that happened, however, David's response was, "Deal gently for my sake with the young man Absalom" (2 Samuel 18:5). There was no spirit of retaliation—only grace. Yet despite all this pain, David never reached out to bring reconciliation. Upon learning of Absalom's death he wept. "The king was deeply moved, and went up to the chamber over the gate, and wept. And as he went, he said, 'O my son Absalom, my son, my son Absalom! Would I had died instead of you, O Absalom, my son, my son'" (2 Samuel 18:33).

Out of all this chaos, pain, and sorrow, David wrote Psalm 3 when he fled from his son Absalom as recorded in 2 Samuel 15:13-29.

O LORD, how my foes have increased!
    How many rise up against me!
Many say of me,
    "God will not deliver him."

But You, O LORD, are a shield around me,
    my glory, and the One who lifts my head.
To the LORD I cry aloud,
    and He answers me from His holy mountain.

I lie down and sleep;
    I wake again, for the LORD sustains me.
I will not fear the myriads
    set against me on every side.

Arise, O LORD!
    Save me, O my God!
Strike all my enemies on the jaw;
    break the teeth of the wicked.
Salvation belongs to the LORD;
    may Your blessing be on Your people.

4

SATAN

The first insurrection

Satan was the first to do it. His revolt speaks volumes about the topic of disloyalty. If there was any doubt about the evil of infidelity, the case is closed: this was the mother of all sins.

The story of Lucifer's fall is described in Isaiah 14 and Ezekiel 28. There is some debate about whether these passages are only speaking about historical figures or if there is a dual application to the kings of Babylon and Tyre plus Satan. The first ten verses of Ezekiel 28 may refer to a human leader, but then the rest of the chapter speaks about an individual that does not seem mortal.

- This is someone who was blameless and sinless (15).
- He was in Eden (13).
- He had "the signet of perfection, full of wisdom and perfect in beauty" (12).
- It seems he had access to heaven (13-14).
- This was a cherub, an angelic being (14).
- His judgment was to be cast to earth (16).

There is a similar pattern in the Isaiah passage. The first portion of the chapter seems to refer to a man, but then verses 12-17 refer to an individual that is other than human. Some might propose that these kings were possessed by Satan. Most presume, however, that these passages describe for us the unparalleled disloyalty of Lucifer.

Verbalizing Discontent

Satan verbalized his thoughts when he said:

I will ascend to heaven; above the stars of God I will set my throne on high; I will sit on the mount of assembly in the far reaches of the north; I will ascend above the heights of the clouds; I will make myself like the Most High. (Isaiah 14:13-14)

We do not know who he was talking to at that point, but he articulated his attempt to take over or at least be equal in position to God.

Betraying Close Relationships

Lucifer illustrates a second characteristic of disloyalty: it assumes some kind of relationship, and often from someone who is close to you.

Scripture tells us that he was an anointed cherub (Ezekiel 28:14). The first time we read about cherubim is in Genesis 3:24 when God drove Adam and Eve out of the garden for their sin. He placed cherubim at the gate to guard them from the tree of life. We also see cherubim in the tabernacle as golden angels on both sides of the mercy seat in the Holy of Holies where the presence of God resided. Cherubim had a privileged proximity to God.

Satan was no ordinary cherub; he was a guardian cherub. There is uncertainty as to what that means, but it would indicate some level of importance and responsibility in relation to God. Perhaps it has something to do with the scripture that says, "I placed you; you were on the holy mountain of God" (Ezekiel 28:14).

A breach in a relationship makes disloyalty so painful. We want to assume colleagues and friends are people on whom we can depend. Realizing that disloyalty can happen with those who are near to us can drive cynicism and distrust in other close relationships. You may be tempted to look over your shoulder and wonder who may be undermining your leadership. One leader who went through a betrayal told me, "I'm having a hard time trusting anyone."

We need to rise above that, however, because true love gives the benefit of the doubt. Paul said one of the characteristics of love is that it "believes all things" (1 Corinthians 13:7). In other words, we are to assume the best about others. At the same time, we should not be taken by surprise if someone turns against us. We must resist cynicism with love.

Destroying Unity

Satan was likely the highest ranked of all angels, but if not, at least he was in the higher echelons of leadership. We know for sure that he was an "anointed guardian cherub" (Ezekiel 28:14). His name Lucifer means "star of the morning." He was not just a rank-and-file angel.

Though he held an exalted position, he did not think it was high enough. Disloyalty is often an attempt to gain more authority, a higher position, and more control. Being the second man in an organizational chart is a challenging position. It requires accepting how God has wired you or patiently awaiting the right time for promotion. It takes character to accept your role and serve in that capacity, but disloyal people are often climbers. They are unhappy with their position and seek to dethrone those who may be in their way.

Alternating Agenda

Obviously then, a disloyal person has his or her own agenda. This was evident with Satan as he aspired to have his own throne and be like God.

Pride is at the core of much that drives the human heart, but it started with Satan himself. "Your heart was proud because of your beauty; you corrupted your wisdom for the sake of your Splendor" (Ezekiel 28:17). Pride will steer a person into irrational and bizarre behavior. That is why maturity is a required qualification for a church leader: "He must not be a recent convert, or he may become puffed up with conceit and fall into the condemnation of the devil" (1 Timothy 3:6).

Imagine having a position that granted access to the presence of God and not being happy with that! It was Satan's aspiration to be at least equal with God or perhaps even to kick God off His throne. He wanted to be like God. It was a power grab. This is the same temptation that he tossed out to Adam and Eve. Although it was his own downfall, he came at them with the same enticement. The human heart has a desire to dethrone God. We call that idolatry, which is simply replacing God with something or someone else.

Sin is deceitful and causes deceit. Disloyal people are confident that their agenda is the right one. Perhaps that is the reason why so many instances of disloyalty are never resolved. Both parties are convinced that they are in the right; otherwise there would be no conflict or severed relationships. Timothy Keiningham says, "The fundamental assumption of disloyalty is that life is better without that relationship. The problem is that to a world of easily shifting loyalties, we are likely to find ourselves surrounded by fair-weather friends."[10]

Here is an interesting observation from Torahclass.com about agendas:

---

10   Timothy Keiningham, Lerzan Aksoy , et al., *Why Loyalty Matters: The Groundbreaking Approach to Rediscovering Happiness, Meaning and Lasting Fulfillment in Your Life and Work*, Benbella Books, Inc., Dallas, TX, 2009, p 76.

Every congregation has its "problem child." Sometimes the person that is a problem has more to do with quirks and flaws (even annoyances) that bother people rather than it being an issue of evil or deception. At other times, the person is clearly behaving in ways that God's Word says he or she shouldn't. Or they disrupt the congregation wanting personal attention or at other times to be an anti-leader. An anti-leader is a person who isn't a good enough leader to assemble their own flock so seeks, instead, to take over that which another has created and led. Satan is an anti-leader. He didn't create anything; but he sought to take over that which God has created. Human anti-leaders are in imitation of Satan even if they don't realize it.[11]

Undermining Authority

Leaders intrinsically have position, authority, and responsibility. Satan wanted position so he could have authority. We don't know if he wanted responsibility, but it comes with the package. It is possible to delegate authority but not responsibility. Ultimately, the leader is responsible for what happens. There is no one else to blame. Even if something has been delegated, the leader is still responsible for the success or failure and needs to own up to it if things don't go well. Position and authority enticed Satan to overthrow God.

A weak leader passes the blame on to others. The disloyal person wants the authority but may not want the responsibility. It is easy to criticize others when you are not responsible for the outcome. In fact, a disloyal person can hide behind the responsibility of others.

In spiritual leadership, like that of a pastor, the boundaries of scripture limit authority. The leader who exercises authority in things not delineated in scripture is either cultic or trending

---

11 https://torahclass.com/new-testament-matthew-lesson-49-ch13/?format=video&lang=en

toward cultic leadership. Corrupt leadership demands obedience from their followers. They want others to come along without question. Scripture has a lot to say about this kind of authoritarianism:

> And Jesus called them to him and said to them, "You know that those who are considered rulers of the Gentiles lord it over them, and their great ones exercise authority over them. But it shall not be so among you. But whoever would be great among you must be your servant, and whoever would be first among you must be slave of all. For even the Son of Man came not to be served but to serve, and to give his life as a ransom for many." (Mark 10:42-45)

> Not that we lord it over your faith, but we work with you for your joy, for you stand firm in your faith. (2 Corinthians 1:24)

> For this reason I write these things while I am away from you, that when I come I may not have to be severe in my use of the authority that the Lord has given me for building up and not for tearing down. (2 Corinthians 13:10)

> Shepherd the flock of God that is among you, exercising oversight, not under compulsion, but willingly, as God would have you; not for shameful gain, but eagerly; not domineering over those in your charge, but being examples to the flock. (1 Peter 5:2-3)

Here is where it takes discernment and self-awareness. What we might label disloyalty may be others simply rejecting overbearing or corrupt leadership. If we experience disloyalty, one of our first reactions should be introspection. As mentioned in the previous chapter, we might be the problem. We may have overstepped the boundaries of authority, and others are simply responding to our inappropriate actions.

Recruiting Others

Satan enlisted others to follow him.

> Now war arose in heaven, Michael and his angels fighting against the dragon. And the dragon and his angels fought back, but he was defeated, and there was no longer any place for them in heaven. And the great dragon was thrown down, that ancient serpent, who is called the devil and Satan, the deceiver of the whole world—he was thrown down to the earth, and his angels were thrown down with him. (Revelation 12:7-9)

This was not a rebellion of one being. He recruited millions of others to join him. According to Revelation 12:4, Satan recruited one third of the angelic beings. Revelation 5:11 (KJV) says there were "ten thousand times ten thousand, and thousands of thousands." If that is taken literally, there were more than 100 million angels who followed him. Alternately, the Greek word *murian* may just refer to an innumerable number. Either way, there was a massive number who got recruited by the Evil One.

If you are experiencing disloyalty, it probably won't be by just one person. Disloyal people don't want to stand by themselves. They need others to rally around them. They obviously believe in their agenda and want others to join them.

Betrayal begins in one's thought life, but know that your betrayer will likely share those thoughts with others, drawing them into their web of discontent. Eventually, others will hear about the falling out, so after attempts for reconciliation have failed, expect the need for damage control. You will probably not be able to extinguish the fire, but you can at least try to dampen it.

The Impact of Disloyalty

Satan's rebellion was the granddaddy of all insurrections because it has impacted billions of people ever since creation. Ev-

43

ery single one of us. The Apostle John writes about Satan's fall as "that ancient serpent called the devil, or Satan, who leads the whole world astray" (Revelation 12:9).

Each of us has been spiritually damaged by the disloyalty of Satan. His rebellion led to the fall of Adam and Eve and as a result "sin came into the world through one man, and death through sin, and so death spread to all men because all sinned" (Romans 5:12). The result is that no person begins life with a relationship to God. The religions of the world are an attempt to repair that severed link to Him. Paul describes this attempt like this: "For, being ignorant of the righteousness of God, and seeking to establish their own, they did not submit to God's righteousness" (Romans 10:3). That verse describes all the religions of the world, in direct contrast to the message of the gospel which says abandon your pursuit of doing enough to gain your own righteousness. Instead, the good news is that Christ died to pay the penalty of our sin and rose from the dead to provide righteousness if we will reach out and accept the free offer of forgiveness of sin.

You will never experience disloyalty of the magnitude of Satan, but any case of disloyalty will undoubtedly devastate your world. All those around you will feel the pain and watch you go through the valley of betrayal. It may crash your ministry if you are not able to handle the situation well. Church splits leave a path of destruction which may take decades to repair. At the least, a case of disloyalty will divert your attention from your work. It will disrupt emotional balance and derail the objectives and mission of your ministry. You will wake in the middle of the night thinking about this instead of the positive forward movement of your ministry. You'll find your mind wandering during the day as this disloyalty dominates your thought life. Sorrow and disappointment will cause you to question your calling. Brace yourself. Disloyalty may damage you.

One of the purposes of this book is to simply alert you to the effects and dynamics of disloyalty so you are not caught by surprise. Knowing the characteristics of disloyalty will arm you to keep perspective in the middle of a storm. Understanding the source of all this will help you have context for the valley of disloyalty.

5

PETER

Repairing disloyalty

One of the amazing facets of God is that He has experienced human life. Not that He needed to come to earth as a man to understand us, but for our benefit, the incarnation helps us to appreciate that He truly understands us. "For we do not have a high priest who is unable to sympathize with our weaknesses, but one who in every respect has been tempted as we are, yet without sin" (Hebrews 4:15).

Additionally, we have a God who doesn't expect us to do things that He has not done. We are to forgive, but He has already done that. We are to show mercy and grace, which God does in abundance. He was tempted. He loved enemies. He empathized. He sacrificed for others. He asks us to send our kids to the mission field, and He also did that (John 3:16). We have a God who is connected and interested.

So when we face disloyalty, God assures us He knows firsthand what that feels like—but in a brutal way like few of us will ever experience. While His incarnation was primarily about death and resurrection, He also showed us how to live. The next two chapters will look at two instances (Peter and Judas) in which Jesus went through gut-wrenching disloyalty. What a great encouragement to know that God feels our pain.

'Fess Up Quickly

The story begins in Matthew 26 as Jesus told his disciples: "You will all fall away because of me this night. For it is written, 'I will strike the shepherd, and the sheep of the flock will be scattered'" (31). In typical fashion, Peter was the first to speak up and say, "Though they all fall away because of you, I will never fall away" (33). When Jesus told him that he would deny him three times before the rooster crowed, Peter dug a deeper hole for himself: "Even if I must die with you, I will not deny you!" (35). The other disciples joined Peter in their vow to remain loyal.

It was not long after that when the soldiers showed up in the Garden of Gethsemane to arrest Jesus. "'But all this has taken place that the Scriptures of the prophets might be fulfilled.' Then all the disciples left him and fled." (56). Disloyalty is such an important topic that Old Testament prophecies included it about Christ. This may be a reference to passages like Zechariah 13:7, Psalm 38:11, and Psalm 88:18. Regardless of which prophets may have seen this coming, it signals to us that disloyalty is to be expected. It is part of life, leadership and ministry. If Jesus faced disloyalty, we should not expect less. When soldiers came to arrest Him, He let them know they were not taking Him by surprise, and all of this was prophesied to happen.

The story continues:

> Then those who had seized Jesus led him to Caiaphas the high priest, where the scribes and the elders had gathered. And Peter was following him at a distance, as far as the courtyard of the high priest, and going inside he sat with the guards to see the end. (57-58)

At first he was standing outside, but then one of the other disciples who had not fled got permission to let Peter come into the courtyard by the fire. As the young lady guarding the door saw Peter, she observed, "You also were with Jesus the Galilean" (69). Peter blurted out, "I do not know what you mean" (70). She obviously didn't believe his denial because a little later this same young lady wouldn't let it go as she again pressed the issue: "This man was with Jesus of Nazareth" (71). This time Peter's response was an oath where he vehemently blurted out, "I do not know the man" (72). Shortly after that, there were some standing around who said, "Certainly you too are one of them, for your accent betrays you" (73). This third denial was even stronger as he lost his composure, screaming curses and swearing, "I do not know the man" (74).

Then the rooster crowed.

It must have been remarkably shrill in the ears of Peter. The very thing that he swore he would never do . . . he just did. It was a shocking awakening to his own weakness and betrayal.

And the Lord turned and looked at Peter. And Peter remembered the saying of the Lord, how he had said to him, "Before the rooster crows today, you will deny me three times." And he went out and wept bitterly. (Luke 22:61-62)

We don't know what kind of look that was. Perhaps it was an I-told-you-so look. Or it may have been pity. Or it could have been condemnation, but probably not. Whatever it was, there were no words needed as Jesus and Peter locked eyes. Peter immediately knew he was guilty. I would like to imagine that it was a look of forgiveness. The point is that Peter immediately grasped what he had just done when he wept bitterly. Remorse and repentance are the positive responses for disloyalty.

Unfortunately, those are not the typical responses of a disloyal person. According to the survey, one-third of the disloyalty events have never been resolved. Almost half of them took over a year to reconcile. That would seem to indicate that often disloyal people are not quick to acknowledge what they have done or to seek reconciliation. We might want to criticize Peter for his denial of Christ, but we should applaud him for being sensitive to his own weakness in sin.

When you sin, it is often easier to ask for forgiveness sooner rather than later. If you say something you should not have said and can catch yourself immediately, it is relatively easy to admit what you just said wrong and ask for forgiveness. If you wait for six days, it becomes more difficult to bring it up and talk about it. If you wait six months, it is awkward to revisit the topic and ask for forgiveness. It's a lot easier if you can immediately admit your fault and seek reconciliation with those you offended.

Never Say Never

One of the big lessons from Peter's experience was that we should not be over-confident. We are all frail and saturated with sin. Our pride might lead us to assume we are above the sin of disloyalty. "I would never do that" is a trap. Peter led the pack of all the disciples who over-promised their loyalty to Christ, yet they all fled.

Peter was the rock, yet he failed. All of us are potentially disloyal. We have been cautioned about this in 1 Corinthians 10:12: "Therefore, let anyone who thinks that he stands take heed lest he fall." Peter had brazenly promised loyalty even to death but quickly found that is easier said than done.

If we can truly embrace the idea that we, too, could be disloyal, it will flavor our response to people when they stab us in the back. Our default reaction is to rise in disdain and anger toward the person offending us. In our arrogance and denial of our own frailty, we posture that we would never do that. But if we understand our own frailty, we will be quick to forgive.

The biblical response is: "Brothers, if anyone is caught in any transgression, you who are spiritual should restore him in a spirit of gentleness. Keep watch on yourself, lest you too be tempted" (Galatians 6:1). Gentleness should characterize our response and attitude. Humility should cause us to be self-aware and admit that we are capable of the same sin. Being stabbed in the back is painful, but it will only add to the throbbing if we act superior. We are all capable of anything.

We should acknowledge the positive side of this disciple. He was bold enough to pull out a sword when surrounded by soldiers. He was courageous enough to follow Jesus into the city when the rest of the disciples fled. He was incredibly audacious to stand around the fire at the high priest's house. Remember that it was Malchus, the servant of the high priest, who lost his ear from Peter's sword. The last place he would have been welcomed at that point was where he could be recognized and arrested.

Common sense would have been to get out of there right away, but Peter had the bravado to stay there for another hour after he was recognized (Luke 22:59). There were officers who shared that fire who could have arrested him at any time. As they were waiting for proceedings to take place in the house, there would have been time for small talk, and it would not be a stretch to imagine the guards and soldiers were processing what they had just heard about Peter. Just a few feet away were the seventy-one members of the Sanhedrin who were strategizing how to get rid of his friend and master and eliminate His followers. Yet Peter hung around.

Look for the Good

The default response is to demonize a disloyal person, and sometimes, as with Judas, it is fair to do so. But there are situations, like Peter's, that should cause us to pause to see the positive side of an individual. The disloyal person may not be as evil as we might presume. One of the ways to process disloyalty toward us is to appreciate the positive characteristics and actions of the individual. They may not be totally corrupt. They are not necessarily our enemy. Frequently, things are not as they appear. There is often another layer if we dig deeper. The situation with Peter's disloyalty is part of a bigger story.

Jesus revealed to Peter that Satan had asked for permission to sift Peter like wheat (Luke 22:32). There was a spiritual battle going on behind the scenes that was not obvious to a casual observer. Jesus could have stopped Satan in his tracks but instead allowed the Evil One to get involved. We find that same scenario in the story of Job where Satan was taunting God. The Lord allowed him to put Job to the test.

One of the greatest testing times of my life was a situation of disloyalty. It was the only time that I ever considered giving up on vocational ministry. Yet in hindsight I can see how critical that stressful event was in my life to prepare me for the next assignment in my life. God allowed me to experience things that prepared me to do a better job in the years ahead. It was part of my schooling even though during the event I could not see or understand that.

That seems to be what is happening here in Peter's life. He experienced the strengthening and grace of God in a high stress situation that flavored his interpersonal relationships for the rest of his life. This undoubtedly prepared him for being a leader in the early church. Jesus said, "But I have prayed for you that your faith may not fail. And when you have turned again, strengthen your brothers" (Luke 22:32). The purpose of this testing was to equip Peter to equip others and to bolster their faith.

The takeaway is this: we should be looking for the good that will come out of the bad. Experiencing disloyalty is excruciating, but ultimately, that experience will elevate our capacity to serve others. God "comforts us in all our affliction, so that we may be able to comfort those who are in any affliction, with the comfort with which we ourselves are comforted by God" (2 Corinthians 1:4). Instead of shrinking into self-pity and defeat, we can leverage the "hits" in our life to catapult us forward in our service to others.

Anticipate Restoration

Though most situations of disloyalty don't end well, we can continue to hold hope for a positive outcome. Peter's experience gives us that hope. One instance of disloyalty does not need to be the end of the relationship. In fact, this event of disloyalty enhanced Peter's commitment and relation to Christ.

After the resurrection, Jesus came walking on the shore to chat with the disciples who had gone back to fishing. Breakfast was on him. It must have been an awkward meal since the backdrop was their abandonment of Jesus on the night of his arrest. I wonder what they talked about. Perhaps it was just small talk about weather and fishing, but then Jesus addressed the elephant in the room.

"Simon, son of John, do you love me more than these?" (John 21:15). Opinions differ as to what the word *these* refers to. Some think Jesus was asking if Peter loved Him more than the other disciples loved Him or if Peter was more loyal to the other disciples. Another possibility is that He was asking Peter if he loved fishing more than ministry. Whatever Jesus meant, it seems that Peter knew it was really a question about loyalty. Three times he assured Jesus that he loved Him, but it seems that Jesus had another point. Each time Peter answered, Jesus commissioned him to service: "Feed my sheep" (John 21:16-18). Jesus was pushing Peter back into a right relationship with Him which would result in effective ministry for the years ahead.

Restoration from failure elevates ministry capacity, deeper commitment, and greater service. It moves us from self-sufficiency to putting the credit on God. Peter would later write:

Whoever speaks, as one who speaks oracles of God; whoever serves, as one who serves by the strength that God supplies—in order that in everything God may be glorified through Jesus Christ. To him belong glory and dominion forever and ever. Amen. (1 Peter 4:11)

Notice that Peter was careful to say that God provides the strength. It is God who should receive the attention. Peter was loyal to God's glory and dominion.

Peter's denial broke him. Gone was the pride and quick tongue. Gone was the unbridled spirit of bravado. That is what brokenness does. Gene Edwards says,

> A quantum leap is taken when someone is "broken." There are many delivery vehicles for brokenness. It may come through a major failure. It could happen because of sickness or persecution. It might be through struggles with raising children. But once a person hits the wall and comes to the end of himself, he is now poised for a new dimension of leadership.[12]

Edwards further writes about this topic in his book *A Tale of Three Kings.*

> God has a university. It is a small school. Few enroll; even fewer graduate. Very, very few indeed. God has this school because he does not have broken men and women. Instead, he has several other types of people. He has people who claim to have God's authority . . . and don't – people who claim to be broken . . . and aren't. And people who do have God's authority, but who are mad and unbroken. And he has, regretfully, a great mixture of everything in between. All these he has in abundance, but broken men and women, hardly at all.[13]

Scripture addresses this issue: "The LORD is near to the brokenhearted and saves the crushed in spirit" (Psalm 34:18) and "The sacrifices of God are a broken spirit; a broken and contrite heart, O God, you will not despise" (Psalm 51:17). This experience prepared Peter for greater ministry. His heart was more tender.

---

12 Paul Seger, *Chief: Leadership Lessons from a Village in Africa,* 2013, p. 85.
13 Gene Edwards, *A Tale of Three Kings,* Tyndale House Publishers, 1980, p 22.

His empathy was more sensitive. His pride was broken so that he could focus on others.

In another example, Jacob ruined his relationship with his brother Esau through his disloyalty. After years of being apart, he headed home, and on that trip he wrestled with an angel until his hip went out of socket. That was a turning point. He was now ready to meet his brother and face restoration. As he shuffled forward, he bowed seven times before his brother. He limped the rest of his life as a continual reminder of his disloyalty, but it changed his capacity for interpersonal relationships.

Peter went on to be a key leader in the early church. In the end, Peter stood good on his commitment to follow Christ even to death. History indicates that Peter was martyred for his faith and chose to be crucified upside down since he was not worthy of dying the same way Jesus did.

Restoration of relationship should be our goal even though our default reaction is to eliminate this person from our life. The story of Peter offers us hope that there can be something positive that emerges from disloyalty.

6

JUDAS ISCARIOT

When a team member turns

Could you imagine Judas Iscariot as the hero of the story? Who in their right mind would elevate Judas to champion status? Yet that is what Don Richardson found among the Sawi people of Papua New Guinea where he served as a missionary. The author of *Peace Child* describes life among these warrior cannibals. After learning their language, he began teaching the life of Christ and finally got to the story of Judas's treachery and betrayal of the Christ.

The people were thrilled with Judas as the hero, not the villain. They applauded him because in the Sawi culture it was a virtue to be deceitful. The cleverest headhunters among them would befriend their victims before killing and eating them. They venerated treachery and disloyalty. This stretches the credulity of our Western minds. We cannot process this kind of thinking . . . yet we can and we do.

Normally, the disloyal person is the hero of his story and is convinced he is right. He views his cause as standing up for what is right. He is a champion in his own eyes because he is correcting the wrongs of a leader. He does not view his treachery as sinful because he believes he is on the right side of wrong. The Sawi people did not see disloyalty and deceit as a moral issue and, in a similar way, a disloyal person believes he is taking the high road.

As the recipient of disloyalty, it is helpful to understand this dynamic. Your antagonist views his cause as righteous. He justifies his betrayal in his own mind because he is advancing a higher cause and fixing what is erroneous. There is something in you that he sees as deficient. Perhaps this is why reconciliation is so difficult. Both the disloyal and the offended are entrenched in their view of the situation.

As mentioned in the chapter about Absalom, your detractor could have indeed been accurate about some deficiency in your life. While the disloyal person may have blown it out of proportion, there could be some truth to his or her accusations. This is one of the most challenging things to do in a disloyalty situation . . . to be objective enough to see the truth and have the grace to accept that the protester deeply believes in his or her cause against you. She may be wrong . . . she may be right . . . he may be part right and part wrong, but ultimately, it will be difficult for you both to be totally objective.

Here is the bottom line: there is potentially a Judas in all of us.

Of Jesus' twelve disciples, "Only Peter gets more lines of coverage from the Gospel writers than does Judas,"[14] says William Klassen. The story begins this way:

> Then one of the twelve, whose name was Judas Iscariot, went to the chief priests and said, "What will you give me if I deliver him over to you?" And they paid him thirty pieces of silver. And from that moment he sought an opportunity to betray him. (Matthew 26:14-16)

---

14   William Klassen, *Judas: Betrayer or Friend of Jesus?*, Fortress Press, 1996.

Actually, the story begins before this plot was laid between Judas and the chief priests. It begins with Jesus choosing him to be one of His disciples despite knowing from the beginning that he would betray him: "Have I not chosen you, the twelve? Yet one of you is a devil!" (John 6:70). Jesus knew ahead of time that things were not right with Judas. Jesus said: "'And you are clean, but not every one of you.' For he knew who was to betray him; that was why he said, 'Not all of you are clean'" (John 13:10-11).

It is difficult to know what to make of this. Perhaps Jesus was signaling to all leaders who would follow that it is highly likely that there may be a disloyal person on your team. Perhaps He is indicating that no team should only have yes-men. Maybe He is modeling to us how to relate to people we don't entirely trust. We do know that this was a fulfilment of prophecy (Psalm 41:9), but that still begs the question of why God planned it this way.

It causes even more consternation when we understand that Judas was not regenerate. Jesus prayed concerning his disciples: "While I was with them, I kept them in your name, which you have given me. I have guarded them, and not one of them has been lost except the son of destruction, that the Scripture might be fulfilled" (John 17:12). Even more outlandish is the fact that Judas was a disciple, yet he was demonized: "Then Satan entered into Judas called Iscariot, who was of the number of the twelve" (Luke 22:3).

Disloyalty is so traumatic that you will begin to wonder if demons are at work or if the occult world is active. As a recipient of disloyalty, you'll be diverted from your main tasks. You'll lose momentum and focus in your mission. Your thoughts throughout the day and in the middle of the night will automatically gravitate toward the problem. You may lose your appetite and sleep become a luxury. Your wife may watch her beloved shrink and implode before her eyes. The joy of the ministry may turn to thoughts of hating your job and resigning. It can be all encompassing and overwhelming. You will think you are getting a sample of hell.

He May Be a Productive Team Member

One of the ironies of disloyalty is that it can be from someone who is a high-functioning team member. Jesus chose Judas to be an active member of the twelve, giving each of them "authority over unclean spirits, to cast them out, and to heal every disease and every affliction" (Matthew 10:1). Judas went out on assignments with the seventy. He went on preaching campaigns with the other disciples (Luke 9:2-7). He helped pass out bread and fish at the feeding of the 5,000. He was there to hear all of Jesus' teaching and preaching. He witnessed miracles of healing. He saw Lazarus rise from the dead. He walked the hundreds of miles with Jesus and spent thousands of hours with Him.

He served as the treasurer for the disciples. Handling money is a significant role with a lot of responsibility that requires trust. You don't ask scoundrels to be the treasurer.

Judas was thought to be such a reliable member of the twelve that none of them suspected him when Jesus mentioned a betrayer in their midst. Instead, they became worried when Jesus said one of them would betray him. They didn't automatically think of Judas. "And as they were eating, he said, 'Truly, I say to you, one of you will betray me.' And they were very sorrowful and began to say to him one after another, 'Is it I, Lord?'" (Matthew 26:21-22). When Jesus told him, "What you are going to do, do quickly" (John 13:27), the others in the room simply thought Jesus was sending Judas on an errand. They did not suspect Judas of betrayal. Years later, Matthew would acknowledge that Judas "was numbered among us and was allotted his share in this ministry" (Acts 1:17). This unregenerate man did ministry shoulder-to-shoulder with the other eleven disciples.

But Judas was not a true follower.

Jesus said to him, "The one who has bathed does not need to wash, except for his feet, but is completely clean. And you are clean, but not every one of you." For he knew who was to betray him; that was why he said, "Not all of you are clean." (John 13:10-11)

Despite all this, Jesus said, "Did I not choose you, the twelve? And yet one of you is a devil" (John 6:70).

It seems incongruous that co-workers or team members would be disloyal when they are key players on the team. Unfortunately, productive team members are not always what they seem to be. Ironically, someone on the pastoral search committee who facilitated and endorsed the calling of a new pastor may be the one who turns against him.

This knowledge can generate cynicism, making it difficult for a leader to trust those around him. Leaders can become paranoid and over-compensate by keeping co-workers at arm's length and preventing the team from becoming high-functioning. Teamwork requires trust. This should not take you by surprise, but leaders must resist the distrust that might emerge from this knowledge.

He May Be a Close Friend

It is amazing that Jesus had a close relationship with Judas despite knowing what he would do. It is difficult enough to handle a co-worker turning against you, but it is even more distressing to have a friend betray you. A Messianic prophecy puts it this way: "Even my close friend in whom I trusted, who ate my bread, has lifted his heel against me" (Psalm 41:9). Jesus gave him the guest-of-honor seat at the last supper, close enough to share a bowl. Jesus treated him with the respect of a friend.

While Jesus loved Judas, that relationship was not reciprocal. The other disciples called Jesus "Lord," but we see Judas calling him "Rabbi" (Matthew 26:25). He addressed him with a formal title—perhaps an acknowledgment that he felt distant in his relationship. Whatever the case, Jesus loved him and that made the separation so painful. "After saying these things, Jesus was troubled in his spirit, and testified, 'Truly, truly, I say to you, one of you will betray me'" (John 13:21).

In my survey, only 7 percent of the respondents said the disloyal person in their life was personally distant in relationship. Almost 27 percent said that this person was extremely close to them. Unfortunately, there is not an easy path around this. It is going to be exceedingly painful when a friend turns against you. Your feelings of disbelief will turn to disappointment which may turn to anger.

The irony is that right in the midst of betrayal, someone can appear to be close and supportive. Judas greeted Jesus with a kiss. In that day, a kiss would be a sign of respect, honor, and brotherly love (Luke 7:45; Romans 16:16; 1 Corinthians 16:20; 2 Corinthians 13:12; 1 Thessalonians 5:26). Yet this act of devotion was brazenly deceitful. Judas was not merely speaking some derogatory words against Jesus; his kiss pronounced a death sentence. Jesus obviously knew that, but He still called him "friend" (Matthew 26:50).

Amazing. That has to be one of the major hurdles when we have been betrayed. How can we treat our adversary as a friend? How do we remain civil? How do we dampen the urge to retaliate? How do we forgive? It is difficult to embrace someone who is stabbing us in the back. This is the ultimate test of our capacity to love.

Check Your Motives

There can be multiple motivations for disloyalty. In Judas's case it was simply a proclivity for riches. In the story of Mary anointing the feet of Jesus, he deflected his true thoughts about Mary by suggesting that the cost of the perfume could have cared for a lot of poor people. But his true motives were "not because he cared about the poor, but because he was a thief, and having charge of the moneybag he used to help himself to what was put into it" (John 12:6).

Immediately after seeing that Jesus operated by a different set of priorities and that Jesus was not going to be the money train he hoped for, "Then Judas Iscariot, who was one of the twelve, went to the chief priests in order to betray him to them" (Mark 14:10). Judas said, "'What will you give me if I deliver him over to you?' And they paid him thirty pieces of silver. And from that moment he sought an opportunity to betray him" (Matthew 26:15-16).

Money, however, isn't the only thing that motivates people to be disloyal. Here are a few other possibilities:

1. Position: Some people simply covet a following.
2. Power: While this is closely connected with position, power may be the driving force. Some have an inordinate need to be in control.
3. Prestige: This may be linked with position and power, but there are those who love the praise of man and will do almost anything to get it.
4. Cause: Disloyal people can sometimes have a higher cause than just position, power, or prestige. They may genuinely seek what they think is correcting a wrong or saving others from the wrong kind of leadership.
5. Values: We all have a hierarchy of priorities for our life, and it may simply be that a disloyal person is driven by a different set of values.
6. Demons: The Gospels say that Satan entered Judas at certain times, and that influenced his decision to betray Jesus. It is possible that the Evil One is attacking your ministry, and this disloyal person is a willing pawn.

While it may not really matter what the motives may be, it is helpful to understand that disloyal people have an agenda. The temptation is to take it personally and be offended, but it is helpful to understand and appreciate that they are probably struggling with other issues in their life. It is not likely they will seek your help in overcoming their misplaced priorities, but if you do get a chance, you may be able to help them advance in their sanctification.

Choose Your Response

Then when Judas, his betrayer, saw that Jesus was condemned, he changed his mind and brought back the thirty pieces of silver to the chief priests and the elders, saying, "I have sinned by betraying innocent blood." They said, "What is that to us? See to it yourself." And throwing down the pieces of silver into the temple, he departed, and he went and hanged himself. (Matthew 27:3-5)

Judas's choice stands in stark contrast to Peter's reaction to his own disloyalty. Judas's betrayal led to Jesus' arrest. Though it brought sorrow to Jesus, Peter's disloyalty did not lead to His death. While Judas had a problem with money, Peter was arrogant and overestimated his courage. Judas had the sin of greed, and Peter had the sin of pride. Yet what a difference in their responses! Both had remorse, but instead of suicide, Peter humbled himself and became an influential leader in the expansion of the Great Commission. The truth will surface eventually in a story of betrayal, and parties involved may realize their sin. At that point there are two paths ahead. One leads to repentance and grace while the other stays entrenched in disloyalty. One act of disloyalty can define and scar a person for life, but there is a way to recover: repent.

7

RUTH

The personification of *hesed*

Enough of the bad examples. After looking at five stories of disloyalty, we will now examine five biblical characters who exemplified loyalty.

These famous words are quoted at thousands of weddings every year:

> For where you go I will go, and where you lodge I will lodge. Your people shall be my people, and your God my God. Where you die I will die, and there will I be buried. May the LORD do so to me and more also if anything but death parts me from you. (Ruth 1:16-17)

Ruth provides for us a classic example of solid commitment through the lens of the Hebrew word *hesed*. But before we look at that word, let's review the setting and the story.

Ruth lived during the time of the Judges. Though a Moabite, she was linked to Israel through Lot, the nephew of Abraham. The Moabites came into existence through an incestuous relationship between Lot and his daughter. Over the years, this nation was a continual irritant to Israel. They were an idolatrous people who worshipped Chemosh, sometimes pictured as a fish god. It was a brutal religion. Scripture calls them "the abomination of Moab" (1 Kings 11:7). One of their rulers "took his oldest son, who would have been the next king, and sacrificed him as a burnt offering on the wall" (2 Kings 3:27). They were such an atrocity to the God of Israel that He cursed them (Isaiah 15-16; Jeremiah 48; Ezekiel 25:8-11; Amos 2:1-3). This story covers more than a decade of a dark time for Israel in which "everyone did what was right in his own eyes" (Judges 17:6). Ruth did not come from a good heritage, but she was a jewel.

Now there was famine in the land of Israel, so a woman named Naomi, her husband, and their two sons moved to Moab (today's Jordan), east of the Dead Sea. While they were there, Naomi's one son married Ruth, and the other married Orpah. At some point, Naomi's husband and both sons died, leaving all three women bereft without a social network.

Naomi eventually decided to return to her home in Bethlehem, six miles south of Jerusalem, because she heard "that the LORD had visited His people in giving them food" (Ruth 1:6). Ruth was faced with a decision of whether to stay in Moab or go with her mother-in-law to her land which she had never known. Three times, Naomi pleaded with her daughters-in-law to stay in Moab—which Orpah did. But Ruth refused saying, "Wherever you go, I will go."

Hesed Defined

The small book of Ruth amplifies a major theological concept entrenched in the Hebrew word *hesed*, found over 250 times in the Old Testament. The first time it's used is in Genesis 19:19, and the last time is in Zechariah 7:9. It is difficult (and some would say impossible) to translate the word into English, but the core idea is loyalty within a relationship.

This word is translated many ways: *kindness, loving-kindness, mercy, compassion, love, grace, goodness, steadfast love, unfailing love, devotion, faithful love, faithfulness* and *loyal.*

Hesed is one of God's chief attributes. Scripture repeatedly says that the Lord abounds in *hesed* (Exodus 34:6; Nehemiah 9:17; Psalm 103:8; Daniel 9:4; Jonah 4:2; Lamentations 3:22). When God met Moses on Mount Sinai, He described Himself this way:

> The LORD, the LORD, a God merciful and gracious, slow to anger, and abounding in steadfast love [*hesed*] and faithfulness, keeping steadfast love [*hesed*] for thousands, forgiving iniquity and transgression and sin, but who will by no means clear the guilty, visiting the iniquity of the fathers on the children and the children's children, to the third and the fourth generation. (Exodus 34:6-7)

Darrel L. Bock observes that *hesed* is "wrapping up in itself all the positive attributes of God: love, covenant faithfulness, mercy, grace, kindness, loyalty–in short, acts of devotion and loving-kindness that go beyond the requirements of duty."[15] It is similar to agape love which concentrates on grace, whereas *hesed* is more focused on mercy.[16] Thus the majority of times we find *hesed* translated as *mercy,* but it is mercy based on a relationship within the context of a commitment.

The poem Psalm 136 drives home this concept, as the same phrase "his steadfast love [*hesed*] endures forever" is repeated 26 times. The Jewish nation could not have sung this song without remembering that God is *hesed*. Singing our theology causes us to remember the words and concepts long after what the preacher says.

---

15 Peter Enns, Tremper Longman III, *Dictionary of the Old Testament: Wisdom, Poetry & Writings,* InterVarsity Press, p. 682.

16 Ed Hindson, Ergun Caner, *The Popular Encyclopedia of Apologetics,* Harvest House Publications, p. 332.

Vine writes:

> In general, one may identify three basic meanings of *hesed*, and these three meanings always interact—strength, steadfastness, and love. Any understanding of *hesed* that fails to suggest all three inevitably loses some of its richness. Love by itself easily becomes sentimentalized or universalized apart from the covenant. Yet strength or steadfastness suggests only the fulfillment of a legal (or similar) obligation. *Hesed* refers primarily to mutual and reciprocal rights and obligations between the parties of a relationship (especially Jehovah and Israel). But *hesed* is not only a matter of obligation but is also of generosity. It is not only a matter of loyalty, but also of mercy. *Hesed* implies personal involvement and commitment in a relationship beyond the rule of law.[17]

Hesed is more than mere emotion because it carries with it the idea of action based on love and commitment to another person. It assumes a relationship. It is often used in connection with God's covenant to His people. N. H. Snaith says:

> The word is used only in cases where there is some recognized tie between the parties concerned. It is not used indiscriminately of kindness in general, haphazard, kindly deeds; God's loving-kindness is that sure love which will not let Israel go. Not all Israel's persistent waywardness could ever destroy it. Though Israel be faithless, yet God remains faithful still. This steady, persistent refusal of God to wash his hands of wayward Israel is the essential meaning of the Hebrew word which is translated loving-kindness [*hesed*].[18]

God wants us to make *hesed* a priority in our lives. Micah 6:8 rises to a 30,000-foot level to give us an overview of the Chris-

---

17 W. E. Vine, *Vine's Complete Expository Dictionary of Old and New Testament Words*, Thomas Nelson, 1996.
18 N.H. Snaith, *The Distinctive Ideas of the Old Testament*, London, 1944, p. 107.

tian walk: "He has told you, O man, what is good; and what does the LORD require of you but to do justice, and to love kindness [*hesed*], and to walk humbly with your God?" This is one of the over-arching concepts to implement in our Christian walk.

The word *hesed* is used more in Psalms than in any other book of the Old Testament. Psalm 23 is probably the most familiar, and the poem crescendos with this concept: "Surely goodness and mercy [*hesed*] shall follow me all the days of my life" (Psalm 23:6). This term became a dominant feature of David's life and thus his psalms. For instance, when he was fleeing in the wilderness he wrote: "O God, You are my God. Earnestly I seek You; my soul thirsts for You. My body yearns for You in a dry and weary land without water . . . because your steadfast love [*hesed*] is better than life" (Psalm 63:1, 3).

This word is rich and complex, and this brief examination of the term doesn't do it justice. Any study of loyalty must include an understanding of *hesed* to round out the definition of the topic.

Hesed in Relationships

Loyalty assumes a relationship, and it sometimes includes a verbalized commitment. Jonathan articulated his loyalty to David. God did so with the nation of Israel. Couples speak their covenant vows at their marriage ceremony. "Its meaning may be summed up as 'steadfast love on the basis of a covenant.' It is employed both of God's attitude towards his people and of theirs to him, the latter especially in Hosea."[19] God prioritizes *hesed* above religious rituals: "For I desire steadfast love [*hesed*] and not sacrifice, the knowledge of God rather than burnt offerings" (Hosea 6:6). When God gave His covenant at Sinai, He referred to it as a "covenant of *hesed*" (Deuteronomy 7:9).

---

19 N. H. Snaith, *The Distinctive Ideas of the Old Testament,* London, 1944, pp. 94–130.

While our English word *loyalty* does not require a verbalized covenant, it assumes some kind of commitment. We assume an employee will be loyal to his employer. Betraying the company to competitors is grounds for being fired. Friendship assumes a person will stand with you whether or not he says he will. Soldiers and politicians swear their allegiance to their country, and every citizen has an unspoken understanding that you don't betray your nation.

Understanding the term *hesed* shines a brilliant light on our understanding of loyalty. It is a firm commitment to (and possibly a covenant in) a relationship that will remain regardless of circumstances. Even when our friends do something bad, we stick with them, not to condone their sin but to be there for them. When someone does wrong, our default should be to extend *hesed* (often translated mercy). He or she may not deserve it, but that is what mercy and grace are all about.

Hesed Is Kindness

Another key facet of *hesed* is kindness. That is why it is often translated *loving-kindness*. Loyalty means you act nicely toward another person. This is action, not just words. David's commitment of loyalty to Jonathan extended beyond his death when David sought out his surviving son, Mephibosheth, to show kindness. "And David said, 'Is there still anyone left of the house of Saul, that I may show him kindness [*hesed*] for Jonathan's sake?'" (2 Samuel 9:1). This ongoing covenant relationship showed itself in practical ways even after the death of a friend.

As I write this today, I was informed that a long-time friend is being brought to court on serious charges. My default reaction is that I don't believe it unless it is proven he did wrong. He gets the benefit of the doubt. Even if he is convicted, he is still my friend, and I'll stand with him through this trial. Kindness is a godly attribute that I want to exhibit as I progress in Christlikeness. It is not something my friend must earn. It may not even be deserved, but I'm going to be loyal.

When the nation of Israel wished they were back in Egypt and turned against Moses, God said, "I will strike them with the pestilence and disinherit them" (Numbers 14:12). Moses began to argue with God that this would be an unwise decision because the nations around would denigrate Him for not being able to bring them into the promised land. Then he shifted to appealing to God's attributes:

> The LORD is slow to anger and abounding in steadfast love, forgiving iniquity and transgression, but he will by no means clear the guilty, visiting the iniquity of the fathers on the children, to the third and the fourth generation. Please pardon the iniquity of this people, according to the greatness of your steadfast love [*hesed*], just as you have forgiven this people, from Egypt until now. (Numbers 14:18-19)

Moses argued for steadfast love and forgiving iniquity, a challenging concept to us because our default reaction to disloyalty is to call down judgment. *Hesed* comes from a root word that means "to bow your head as a gesture of courtesy, kindness, grace, and benevolence." That is hard to do when the knife is still in your back.

Hesed Means Others First

The word *hesed* is used three times in the book of Ruth. The first was when Ruth followed her mother-in-law (1:8). She had every right to stay in Moab, start over, and seek a new spouse from within her people; but as widow and outsider, she made the commitment to move to Bethlehem and risk being single the rest of her life. The second instance was when Naomi blessed Boaz for his kindness (2:20).

The third use of *hesed* is when Boaz said, "May you be blessed by the LORD, my daughter. You have made this last kindness [*hesed*] greater than the first in that you have not gone after young men, whether poor or rich" (3:10). He noticed Ruth put others before herself.

Putting others first is at the core of loyalty. Ruth called judgment on herself if she were ever disloyal to Naomi (1:17). She was radically committed to serving her. This may seem extreme to us when we think of our own loyal relationships. It is, however, the basis of marriage: "Husbands, love your wives, as Christ loved the church and gave himself up for her" (Ephesians 5:25). Husbands are to put their wives first, even to death.

While we can understand this in a marriage, this also applies to friendships: "Greater love has no one than this, that someone lay down his life for his friends" (John 15:13). That is radical stuff, but it demonstrates the seriousness of *hesed* or loyalty in our relationships.

"I have your back" is the opposite of "stabbed in the back." Loyalty vs. disloyalty. It has been a joy to have co-workers over the years who had my back. For twenty-seven years I served as the director of a mission agency, and during all those years, Steve Rygh served as the CFO for the organization. It was wonderful to have him on the leadership team and know that he was looking out for my best. I could relax knowing that he would not undermine my leadership and that he would alert me to undercurrents which might adversely affect me.

His loyalty included his freedom to let me know when he didn't agree with something I was about to do, but then it extended further to support my decision even though it wasn't his preference. That is a classic illustration of putting others first. Steve is an example of so many others in my life and ministry (too many to name) who have blessed me with a *hesed* relationship. I've been fortunate. It has made my work environment a pleasure.

Putting others first begins with being willing to go to that person first without talking to others. Matthew 18:15 gives us instruction on how to handle offenses: "If your brother sins against you, go and tell him his fault, between you and him alone." While the context here is sin, there is a general principle that we keep things in as small a circle as possible. The natural tendency is to talk to others first before approaching the offender. The same is true about loyalty. Your loyal friend will approach you first without talking to others.

70

To be a loyal person also means that you will leave the comfort of silence and speak up when you see potential harm in your friend's circumstances. It is awkward to broach delicate issues. It is much easier to excuse ourselves that it is "not our business." Yet a loyal person is quick to warn about danger.

Even though *hesed* is others-oriented, when we put others first, blessings roll back on us. Scripture gives us a promise that "The man who is kind [*hesed*] benefits himself, but a cruel man hurts himself" (Proverbs 11:17), and "Whoever pursues righteousness and kindness will find life, righteousness, and honor" (Proverbs 21:21).

Rest of the Story

Ruth moved to Bethlehem, the most famous birthplace in history, and ended up marrying Boaz. Their son Obed became the father of Jesse, who became the father of David, making Ruth the great-grandmother of this legendary king. She became part of the lineage of Jesus. She could never have imagined that one decision could have ramifications that would last thousands of years and impact millions of people. Our loyalty today may have multi-generational results. We may never know until heaven the backstory of our loyalty or disloyalty to others.

This story also illustrates grace and mercy, key components of *hesed*. Here was a widow from an enemy nation who was reaping wheat from fields where the people's racism would naturally reject her. Yet in this hostile environment, Ruth found grace. She received that grace from someone who was a product of grace because Boaz's mother was Rahab the prostitute who helped the spies in Jericho. He had undoubtedly heard the story many times of how God had granted grace to a harlot. Could it be that this flavored his commitment to *hesed* and foreshadowed Jesus to serve as the kinsman redeemer? Being a recipient of grace made him observant of the need for grace in others.

Boaz said:

All that you have done for your mother-in-law since the death of your husband has been fully told to me, and how you left your father and mother and your native land and came to a people that you did not know before. The LORD repay you for what you have done, and a full reward be given you by the LORD, the God of Israel, under whose wings you have come to take refuge! (2:11-12)

Following the levirate marriage laws of Israel meant Boaz diluted what he would provide for his heirs, since Ruth's first-born male would have claim to Naomi's inheritance. This was sacrifice and grace on the part of Boaz. This story certainly moves us to be gracious in our relationships, granting to others what they don't really deserve.

Ruth is a fitting example to us that loyalty (and thus mercy and grace) comes with a price. Ruth was willing to do that, and we have been talking about her ever since. I wonder if this influenced her great-great-grandson, Solomon, to encourage his son: "Let not steadfast love [hesed] and faithfulness forsake you; bind them around your neck; write them on the tablet of your heart" (Proverbs 3:3). Hesed was part of his heritage.

8

ABIGAIL
Loyal to difficult people

Whether you are a country music fan or not, you've probably heard of Tammy Wynette who is famous for her song "Stand By Your Man." The popularity of this song is a bit incongruous on several levels, the first of which is she was married five times. Second, the sentiment of the song is certainly not politically correct in an environment of women's rights. Despite that, it became number one on the country music charts, earned her a Grammy, and remains the biggest song of Wynette's career. Some of the words are:

> You'll have bad times and he'll have good times
> Doin' things that you don't understand
> But if you love him, oh, be proud of him
> 'Cause after all, he's just a man.

But if you love him, you'll forgive him
Even though he's hard to understand
And if you love him, oh, be proud of him
'Cause after all, he's just a man.

"I've tried through the years to analyze why people have liked the song and kept demanding the song," Wynette said. "The only thing I can come up with is that it's what they really would have liked to have happen in their lives. Maybe it's only a fantasy. Maybe it's something they dream about that never works for them."[20] She is probably correct. Everyone would like to have loyal people in their lives. We want to be loved unconditionally despite our weaknesses or sins.

But how do you remain loyal to people when they don't deserve it? How do you stand by someone who has sinned or is clearly in the wrong? How does loyalty fit when someone has serious character flaws? How do you relate to a leader who is not worthy?

Over half of those who responded to the survey answered in the affirmative to the following question: Have you ever been a part of an organization where unhealthy loyalty (not being allowed to question the leader, i.e., "worshipping" the leader, etc.) was practiced? That most of the respondents were Christian leaders is disconcerting. We find difficult leaders not just in the secular world but also in the church and Christian organizations.

While "Stand by your man" is not our natural reaction, it is a component of loyalty which Abigail dramatically illustrates.

The story begins with David camping in the wilderness of Paran, located on the Sinai Peninsula. David was fleeing from King Saul who was motivated by insecurity and obsessed with jealousy. Saul knew David was popular and that he would someday be king, and he sought to kill him. That death threat had David fleeing for his life, cave dwelling a long way from Jerusalem in the area where Israel had wandered in the wilderness.

---

20 https://www.latimes.com/archives/la-xpm-1991-01-21-ca-422-story.html

Other misfits and malcontents joined him in the desert. 1 Samuel says:

> David departed from there and escaped to the cave of Adullam. And when his brothers and all his father's house heard it, they went down there to him. And everyone who was in distress, and everyone who was in debt, and everyone who was bitter in soul, gathered to him. And he became commander over them. And there were with him about four hundred men. (22:1-2)

Even though they were a motley group of men, David was able to lead them and corral them into guarding some sheepherders in the desert.

One of the recipients of their protection was Nabal, a wealthy property owner who had a thousand goats and three thousand sheep. We are told that he was harsh and badly behaved. His wife Abigail, however, was a gem. This was a case of Beauty and the Beast.

David Guznik quotes Clarke as saying: "The fact that he was of the house of Caleb may also be an unflattering description of Nabal because Caleb means dog, and to be of the house of a dog was no compliment."[21] This malevolent man was married to Abigail.

The story takes place during a sheep-shearing festival, a time for feasting and revelry. Thus it was not unreasonable that David sent ten of his men to visit Nabal.

> David said to the young men, "Go up to Carmel, and go to Nabal and greet him in my name. And thus you shall greet him: 'Peace be to you, and peace be to your house, and peace be to all that you have. I hear that you have shearers. Now your shepherds have been with us, and we did them no harm, and they missed nothing all the time they were in Carmel. Ask your young men, and they will tell you. Therefore let my

---

21 https://enduringword.com/bible-commentary/1-samuel-25/

young men find favor in your eyes, for we come on a feast day. Please give whatever you have at hand to your servants and to your son David.'" (25:5-8)

Nabal's response was absolutely not!

Who is David? Who is the son of Jesse? There are many servants these days who are breaking away from their masters. Shall I take my bread and my water and my meat that I have killed for my shearers and give it to men who come from I do not know where? (25:10-11)

His reaction enraged David to the point that he armed four hundred of his men and headed off to take things by force and kill Nabal and all the men surrounding him.

Now David had said, "Surely in vain have I guarded all that this fellow has in the wilderness, so that nothing was missed of all that belonged to him, and he has returned me evil for good. God do so to the enemies of David and more also, if by morning I leave so much as one male of all who belong to him." (25:21-22)

In the meantime, one of Nabal's servants told Abigail what had just happened.

Then Abigail made haste and took two hundred loaves and two skins of wine and five sheep already prepared and five seahs of parched grain and a hundred clusters of raisins and two hundred cakes of figs, and laid them on donkeys. And she said to her young men, "Go on before me; behold, I come after you." But she did not tell her husband Nabal. (25:18-19)

When Abigail met David on the road, she got off her donkey, bowed before David and made an amazing speech:

On me alone, my lord, be the guilt. Please let your servant speak in your ears, and hear the words of your servant. Let not my lord regard this worthless fellow, Nabal, for as his name is, so is he. Nabal is his name, and folly is with him. But I your servant did not see the young men of my lord, whom you sent. Now then, my lord, as the Lord lives, and as your soul lives, because the Lord has restrained you from bloodguilt and from saving with your own hand, now then let your enemies and those who seek to do evil to my lord be as Nabal. And now let this present that your servant has brought to my lord be given to the young men who follow my lord. Please forgive the trespass of your servant. For the Lord will certainly make my lord a sure house, because my lord is fighting the battles of the Lord, and evil shall not be found in you so long as you live. If men rise up to pursue you and to seek your life, the life of my lord shall be bound in the bundle of the living in the care of the Lord your God. And the lives of your enemies he shall sling out as from the hollow of a sling. And when the Lord has done to my lord according to all the good that he has spoken concerning you and has appointed you prince over Israel, my lord shall have no cause of grief or pangs of conscience for having shed blood without cause or for my lord working salvation himself. And when the Lord has dealt well with my lord, then remember your servant. (25:24-31)

We will come back to this speech shortly, but first, let's finish the story and then make some observations and applications about loyalty. As a result of Abigail's intervention, David backed down and returned to his desert dwelling with gratitude to Abigail for what she had done. He acknowledged her actions had saved him from reckless murder. In the meantime, Nabal was throwing a party and got drunk so was unaware of what Abigail had just done—until the next morning when she told him. The news was so shocking it appears he had a heart attack, and he died ten days later.

This is an intriguing story when viewed through the lens of loyalty. Nabal would have been a hard person to love, and we might wonder how these two ever ended up getting married when "The woman was discerning and beautiful, but the man was harsh and badly behaved" (25:3). It may be that this was an arranged marriage, and Abigail was making the best of it. Or it might be that Nabal started out well and was a great guy when they got married, but his character deteriorated over the years. Whichever is the case, Abigail is to be commended for her commitment to a difficult man. We don't know anything else about her except what is written in 1 Samuel 25 and 1 Chronicles 3:1, but her example in this one story helps to frame our thinking about the topic of loyalty. Here is what we learn.

She Was Loyal

It would seem impossible for Abigail to love a man like Nabal unless we view the story through the grid of *agape* love, a commitment of the will. She got a raw deal in her marriage, but she is to be applauded for continuing to live with him. Further, she did what she could to protect him by compensating for his surly attitude and taking food to David as a peace offering. She identified herself with her husband and was willing to take the blame: "She fell at his feet and said, 'On me alone, my lord, be the guilt'" (25:24).

Loyalty is driven by love for others. If a condition for love is the other person's perfection, then none of us would ever be loyal. Thus the issue is sometimes whether someone is bad or really bad. What degree of badness would justify love turning to hate? How bad does someone need to be before disloyalty is appropriate? Loyalty should not be based on how good someone is—which leads us to the next point.

She Was Realistic

Being loyal does not mean you are oblivious to the faults of others. Abigail was brutally forthright in describing her husband to David as a "worthless fellow, Nabal, for as his name is, so is he. Nabal is his name, and folly is with him" (25:25). She knew exactly what kind of man she married. She was not naïve or oblivious or in denial. She was objective about Nabal. Yet despite all this, she was loyal.

How many times have we observed an offended wife stand by the side of her adulterous husband? It is not that she agrees with or denies his infidelity but, rather, she is remaining loyal. In many court cases, witnesses will side with the defendant even though they know the truth. They are not denying the truth; they are simply being loyal. Loyalty does not mean we ignore the obvious. The sin and weakness of an individual is not the determining factor for our loyalty.

She Was Brave

Loyalty means you get involved. While the default position might be to stay in the shadows like Peter, loyal people put themselves on the line for the person they love. We would have understood and given grace if Abigail had remained passive and watched Nabal get what he deserved. She might have even rejoiced in the justice her husband would have received through the hand of David. Instead, she was proactive, decisive, and brave. She immediately realized what was at stake and what she should do.

She was brave to take the initiative to solve the problem even though it could have turned out badly for her from her husband. She was brave to head straight toward 400 men on the warpath. David had threatened to kill all the men. She could have assumed that her neck was also on the line and that David would dispatch her life first as he stormed toward Nabal's camp. This was one fearless lady.

Loyalty requires bravery. It means standing up for someone and potentially receiving the backlash that is aimed at the other person. It is easier to step back and let things take their course and not get involved. But loyalty means that we stand as one with that person, both in the good times and the bad times. It may be that, like Abigail, we remain composed and come up with a plan to help calm a volatile situation. It may mean taking the brunt of rejection and retaliation.

She Was Wise

Loyalty does not require silence. In fact, the opposite is true. Loyal people speak the truth to others. Abigail told Nabal exactly what she had done.

> And Abigail came to Nabal, and behold, he was holding a feast in his house, like the feast of a king. And Nabal's heart was merry within him, for he was very drunk. So she told him nothing at all until the morning light. In the morning, when the wine had gone out of Nabal, his wife told him these things, and his heart died within him, and he became as a stone. (25:36-37)

Scripture clearly states that honest communication builds trust. "Faithful are the wounds of a friend; profuse are the kisses of an enemy" (Proverbs 27:6).

Abigail's actions exuded wisdom. She approached David in a spirit of humility when she could have been aggressive like her husband. She understood that "a soft answer turns away wrath" (Proverbs 15:1), and she diffused a tense circumstance. This was a delicate situation where David might have wanted to save face in front of 400 of his men, but she was able to talk him down off the ledge of his anger. She helped him think through the ramifications of his proposed actions against Nabal and how it would be a point of regret when he became king. Wisdom threaded its way through her entire speech. Honest, forthright communication is the mark of a loyal person.

She Trusted God

We don't know how long Abigail had been in this relationship with a difficult man, but it is evident that she trusted God in the middle of these bad circumstances. She told David not to kill Nabal because God would take care of things. David later acknowledged this when he said, "Blessed be the LORD who has avenged the insult I received at the hand of Nabal, and has kept back his servant from wrongdoing. The LORD has returned the evil of Nabal on his own head" (1 Samuel 25:39). Paul writes about this principle in Romans: "Beloved, never avenge yourselves, but leave it to the wrath of God, for it is written, 'Vengeance is mine, I will repay, says the Lord'" (Romans 12:19).

1 Peter 3 addresses the issue of wives who have difficult or unbelieving husbands.

Likewise, wives, be subject to your own husbands, so that even if some do not obey the word, they may be won without a word by the conduct of their wives, when they see your respectful and pure conduct. Do not let your adorning be external—the braiding of hair and the putting on of gold jewelry, or the clothing you wear—but let your adorning be the hidden person of the heart with the imperishable beauty of a gentle and quiet spirit, which in God's sight is very precious. For this is how the holy women who hoped in God used to adorn themselves, by submitting to their own husbands. (1-5)

Obedience to that passage is extremely difficult. Meekness is not a natural response to difficult people, yet Peter instructs wives to win over their husbands by actions, not by words. They are to trust God to work things out. That takes faith.

Abigail provides for us a framework for being loyal when someone is not worthy of allegiance. It is possible that we may be thrust into a working relationship with a repulsive person or a tyrannical boss. It might be that you have some impossible relatives. Your spouse may have taken a wrong turn. A longtime friend may have done evil. If we are going to be loyal to a difficult person, it means that we live in the real world and understand what is going on. It means we are brave enough to speak up. It means we will be wise and honest with people, and it means we will ultimately leave it up to God to bring justice.

9

PAUL

The pain of abandonment

2 Timothy 1:15 must be one of the saddest verses in scripture: "You are aware that all who are in Asia turned away from me." This is the Apostle Paul's last letter written at the end of his life and ministry. The last words people speak are important to us, and it is poignant that disloyalty is the topic on his mind before his death. This was no way to end an exceptional life.

Possibly thousands were affected by Paul's gospel ministry during his lifetime, and for the last 2000 years, millions have been impacted. We know of forty-one men who joined his missionary team at one time or other. He started multiple churches, and the gospel penetrated previously unreached areas. After all this success he should have been able to rest comfortably in the arms of his loyal supporters. Instead, he sits alone in prison writing these words as he awaits his court date. This was an inglorious way to end his ministry.

Though we cannot know their motives, it appears that some wanted to distance themselves from this prisoner. Identifying with him could have resulted in persecution by the Roman government. Perhaps that is why Paul admonished Timothy: "Therefore do not be ashamed of the testimony about our Lord, nor of me his prisoner, but share in suffering for the gospel by the power of God" (2 Timothy 1:8).

This was not the only instance in which Paul had experienced disloyalty. Here are a few of them:

Demas, in love with this present world, has deserted me and gone to Thessalonica. Crescens has gone to Galatia, Titus to Dalmatia. Luke alone is with me. (2 Timothy 4:10-11)

Alexander the coppersmith did me great harm; the Lord will repay him according to his deeds. (2 Timothy 4:14)

At my first defense no one came to stand by me, but all deserted me. (2 Timothy 4:16)

When Paul wrote that Demas had left him, he used the word *deserted* which means "to utterly abandon, leaving someone in a dire situation."[22] Louw and Nida define it this way: "to desert or forsake a person and thus leave that individual uncared for."[23] The Greek word, however, is stronger than the English word. It is made up of three words: λειπω (to leave), κατα (down), and ἐν (in). It means "to forsake one who is in a set of circumstances that are against him."[24] It was a cruel blow to Paul.

This is the same word used by Jesus on the cross: "And about the ninth hour Jesus cried out with a loud voice, saying '*Eli,*

22 John MacArthur Jr., ed., *The MacArthur Study Bible*, electronic ed., Word Publishing, Nashville, TN, 1881, 1997.

23 Johannes P. Louw and Eugene Albert Nida, *Greek-English Lexicon of the New Testament: Based on Semantic Domains,* United Bible Societies, New York, 1996, p. 464.

24 Kenneth S. Wuest, *Wuest's Word Studies from the Greek New Testament: For the English Reader,* Vol. 8, Eerdmans, Grand Rapids, 1997, p. 164.

Eli, lema sabachthani?' that is, 'My God, my God, why have you forsaken me?'" (Matthew 27:46). We all crave relationships with people we can trust. We love the loyalty of others. Oprah Winfrey put it this way: "Lots of people want to ride with you in the limo, but what you want is someone who will take the bus with you when the limo breaks down."[25]

Experiencing disloyalty is a nasty experience, and Paul ended his life with an avalanche. Despite this, however, he remained faithful and loyal. The last verses Paul ever wrote will help us to see how he managed his own loyalty and the disloyalty of others. The rest of this chapter will take a closer look at the context and applications of 2 Timothy 4 as it relates to this theme.

Expect Disloyalty

Paul had experienced an inconceivable litany of hardships in his life.

Five times I received at the hands of the Jews the forty lashes less one. Three times I was beaten with rods. Once I was stoned. Three times I was shipwrecked; a night and a day I was adrift at sea; on frequent journeys, in danger from rivers, danger from robbers, danger from my own people, danger from Gentiles, danger in the city, danger in the wilderness, danger at sea, danger from false brothers; in toil and hardship, through many a sleepless night, in hunger and thirst, often without food, in cold and exposure. (2 Corinthians 11:24-27)

All these trials were physical, but he ended this list mentioning the mental anguish he suffered. "And, apart from other things, there is the daily pressure on me of my anxiety for all the churches" (2 Corinthians 11:28). He experienced fracturing of a

---

25 Allen Blaine, *When People Throw Stones*, Kregel, Grand Rapids, 2005, p. 94.

church he planted because of divided loyalties. To the church at Corinth, he wrote:

> I appeal to you, brothers, by the name of our Lord Jesus Christ, that all of you agree, and that there be no divisions among you, but that you be united in the same mind and the same judgment. For it has been reported to me by Chloe's people that there is quarreling among you, my brothers. What I mean is that each one of you says, "I follow Paul," or "I follow Apollos," or "I follow Cephas," or "I follow Christ." Is Christ divided? Was Paul crucified for you? Or were you baptized in the name of Paul? (1 Corinthians 1:10-13)

It is one thing to go through physical pain, but to experience abandonment by friends and co-workers at the end of a life may be more excruciating. Notice in the middle of this list of hardships Paul mentions "danger from false brothers." Apparently this was not the first time he had been betrayed. It was part of life and ministry for him, and he warned Timothy in this chapter to expect it.

> For the time is coming when people will not endure sound teaching, but having itching ears they will accumulate for themselves teachers to suit their own passions, and will turn away from listening to the truth and wander off into myths. As for you, always be sober-minded, endure suffering, do the work of an evangelist, fulfill your ministry. (2 Timothy 4:3-5)

If 85 percent of the leaders in my survey indicated they experienced disloyalty, there is a good chance we will all walk through that valley at some time in our life. One of the keys to handling disloyalty is to be forewarned and expect it to happen. None of us are immune.

Leadership is a heavy burden of responsibility to provide direction for others. There is a price to pay for leading, however, and disloyalty may be one of them. That thought should not paralyze leaders, nor should it stop someone from assuming a leadership role. It is merely one of the items that needs to be considered as you "count the cost" before stepping into a leadership role. We might think that good leaders would not experience betrayal, but even the most perfect leader in history experienced it. Jesus had Judas. It is not a matter of "if" we get hurt, but "when."

Reading this book may be discouraging to an emerging leader, but it seems appropriate to warn others of disloyal people. Paul did that. "Alexander the coppersmith did me great harm; the Lord will repay him according to his deeds. Beware of him yourself, for he strongly opposed our message" (2 Timothy 4:14-15). Part of the role of leadership is to warn others to anticipate disloyalty, and Paul didn't shy away from naming the individual.

Be Quick to Forgive

A second lesson from Paul in the final chapter of his life is about forgiveness. His words "may it not be charged against them" (2 Timothy 4:16) echo Christ's final words on the cross: "Father, forgive them, for they know not what they do" (Luke 23:34). From His position on the cross, He watched soldiers gambling away His clothing, felt crowds gawking, heard them mocking, and recognized those who had spit on Him, whipped Him, jerked out His beard, and crowned Him with thorns. Perhaps some of His disciples were in the distance. Any or all of these may have been in His thoughts as He said those words, yet we know all would be recipients of His grace and forgiveness. Despite all this betrayal, He did not want the Father to inflict justice on them. He gave us a model for when we have experienced disloyalty. We are commanded to forgive as Christ forgave us (Ephesians 4:32). We have no right to hold a grudge or seek retaliation. Grace and mercy should be our mindset towards those who have offended us.

Paul forgave those who failed to stand with him. It is not clear whether the offenders had asked for forgiveness, but that didn't matter . . . Paul forgave. Forgiving is difficult when we have been severely wounded. It is even more difficult to keep from retaliating. We are instructed to "not repay anyone evil for evil" (Romans 12:17). Our natural inclination is to strike back, either physically or verbally, at someone who has stabbed us in the back. Yet we see none of that in this chapter about disloyalty.

Disloyalty hurts our feelings. Most of the time it is someone we have befriended, and it is at first inconceivable that "that" person would do us harm. We invested ourselves in that relationship and probably trusted him or her. In the case of an employment situation, it is disappointing that someone who is receiving salary from the company or organization would turn against it. The youth pastor who splits the church was probably brought into that position by the pastor he now turns against. That hurts. Extending forgiveness is one way to help heal the hurt.

Seek Companionship

The context of 2 Timothy chapter 4 intensifies Paul's cry for Timothy to come see him. He prefaced his comments about abandonment by asking Timothy to "do your best to come to me soon" (9). In the isolation and loneliness of a damp prison cell, he craved seeing a familiar face. After fifteen years of working together, he saw in Timothy a person he could trust. With nothing to do but wait in that dungeon, the hours seemed like days.

After talking about those who had abandoned him, Paul repeated his plea: "Do your best to come before winter" (21). If Timothy didn't make it before winter, months could pass before the sailing season started again, that would make it possible for Timothy to get there. That felt intolerable. Significantly, some of the last words Paul penned were a cry for companionship.

It may be obvious that the cure for loneliness is to have people surround you. Though some people or animals may prefer solitude when injured, companionship is what they need. Rogue elephants who have been pushed out of the herd go on a rampage. Being with other elephants seems to bring some normality in old bulls, but when they are by themselves, they go wild and dangerously unpredictable, attacking anything that comes in their way, even killing humans.

One of my mentors observed that most leaders are insecure. That didn't make sense to me at the time, but since he had a lifetime of interacting with high-profile leaders, I accepted his analysis. He told me he had just resigned from a key position in a high-profile church that was pastored by a nationally known individual. He found working for an insecure pastor an intolerable situation.

Something that will accelerate self-doubting even further is to experience disloyalty. It is difficult to be objective about your situation and who you are. You lose self-awareness. Succumbing to insecurity will severely damage your leadership potential. You need the objectivity that trusted friends can bring to you.

The prophet Elijah failed to seek companions and became suicidal (1 Kings 19:4). Sitting beside a brook, he asked God to take his life. This depression took place right after seeing astonishing success. He prayed for rain, and it did. He called for fire from heaven, and it came. He took on 850 pagan prophets in a showdown and won. So what was the problem? First, he did what we just talked about . . . he sought solitude and fled to a remote destination. His complaint was:

"I have been very jealous for the LORD, the God of hosts. For the people of Israel have forsaken your covenant, thrown down your altars, and killed your prophets with the sword, and I, even I only, am left, and they seek my life, to take it away." (1 Kings 19:10)

One of the things he failed to acknowledge was all his successes: massive revival in the nation of Israel—a prophet's dream. He failed to count his blessings. Part of the solution to his depression was to realize there were still 7000 others in Israel who would stand by him (1 Kings 19:18). Companionship was part of the cure.

In this 2 Timothy 4 passage, the Apostle Paul processed disloyalty differently from Elijah. While being aware of his impending death, he seemed positive and upbeat, rejoicing in God. He remembered the blessing of friendship and comradery of co-workers like Priscilla and Aquila whom he first met in Corinth and later "risked their necks for my life" (Romans 16:4). He remembered the personal support he received from Onesiphorus when he was in Ephesus and how, at the time, he was not ashamed of his chains. He recalled that co-workers like Erastus were still there in Ephesus. Though he had to leave him to recuperate in Miletus, he remembered Trophimus.

It was therapy for Paul to remember there were still many loyal people in his life. Don't let one person's disloyalty dominate your world. Experiencing disloyalty has a way of taking over your life. All the good things and the good people in your life fade into the background because all you can think about is this one instance of disloyalty. You wake in the middle of the night thinking about it. You daydream about it. You find it hard to focus on other things because the pain of disloyalty controls your thoughts. When that happens, seek companionship.

Stay Focused on Your Calling

Distraction is one of the most frequent results of betrayal. A case of disloyalty will derail your goals and initiatives and distort your focus on your main tasks. All you can think about is your personal pain and broken relationships as they dominate your waking moments. Disloyalty is like a detour in the road that forces you away from the main highway of your life's work and primary mission in life. It is so gut-wrenching that everything else dulls to gray while your stab wounds throb with pain.

So what do you do when this happens? Again, we go to Paul in 2 Timothy 4 and his comments at the end of his life. He starts off this chapter by urging Timothy to stay focused on the main things.

> I charge you in the presence of God and of Christ Jesus, who is to judge the living and the dead, and by his appearing and his kingdom: preach the word; be ready in season and out of season; reprove, rebuke, and exhort, with complete patience and teaching. (1-2)

The context here is especially poignant. He makes this statement right before saying there will be people who will abandon you and the faith (3-4).

As he wrote those words to Timothy, he felt the nagging pain that disloyal co-workers had abandoned him. Yet he stayed focused on the fundamental issues of the work of the ministry. Though difficult, we must stay the course in the middle of the rapids. That assumes you know what your main things are. If you don't know, work on that right now as you prepare for rough waters ahead.

The second thing Paul does in this chapter is to take a self-inventory. While we cannot control how others are acting, we can make sure we are on the right course. Notice the number of times Paul uses the word *I* or *me* in these three verses. It seems he is saying it doesn't matter how others act or react—he is concerned about his own actions and a clear conscience. Managing yourself is critical to steering through the disloyalty of others.

For I am already being poured out as a drink offering, and the time of my departure has come. I have fought the good fight, I have finished the race, I have kept the faith. Henceforth there is laid up for me the crown of righteousness, which the Lord, the righteous judge, will award to me on that day, and not only to me but also to all who have loved his appearing. (6-8)

We may be tempted to succumb to frustration and discouragement, but Paul's example is to do some self-examination. Instead of focusing on your betrayer's actions, make sure you are ready to meet God with a clear conscience.

The third thing Paul does is focus on the future. While sitting in a prison cell, Paul was planning for the days ahead rather than wallowing in the present or the past. This is indicated in phrases like:

Do your best to come to me soon. (9)

When you come, bring the cloak that I left with Carpus at Troas, also the books, and above all the parchments. (13)

The Lord will rescue me from every evil deed and bring me safely into his heavenly kingdom. (18)

Even though he knew his days were numbered, Paul was looking forward to seeing his friend Timothy. He was concerned about life-long learning as he requested "the books and the parchments." At a time when reading and study would have seemed unimportant, Paul was driven by a desire "that I may know him and the power of his resurrection, and may share his sufferings, becoming like him in his death" (Philippians 3:10). In the middle of his pain of abandonment, he was still moving forward into the future with positive goals.

Trust in God

While "trust God" may seem to be a trite and often repeated phrase, it was the bedrock of Paul's stability and tenacity at this low point in his life. Here is what he said:

But the Lord stood by me and strengthened me, so that through me the message might be fully proclaimed and all the Gentiles might hear it. So I was rescued from the lion's mouth. The Lord will rescue me from every evil deed and bring me safely into his heavenly kingdom. To him be the glory forever and ever. Amen. (17-18)

When people disappoint us, it is critical that we place our trust in God as One who "will never leave you nor forsake you" (Hebrews 13:5). Even our best friends will at some time disappoint us, so it is critical to have our stability anchored in God, not in others. The amazing thing is that "if we are faithless, he remains faithful" (2 Timothy 2:13). It is comforting to have at least one relationship in our lives that we can count on 100 percent.

Ultimately the way we are going to make it through the events of disloyalty in our lives is to have a faith that is secured in the One who will never be disloyal.

10

JONATHAN
Caught in the middle

During World War II over 100,000 US citizens of Japanese descent were confined to internment camps. The attack on Pearl Harbor immediately raised suspicions as to where their loyalties were. This heartless and unfair treatment of US citizens later resulted in apologies and reparations through the Civil Liberties Act of 1988. That legislation admitted the government actions were based on racism.

Competing loyalties can put us into some awkward situations. Loyalty to a group such as a nation, a company, a church, or a political party complicates our relationships. If countries are at peace with each other, holding dual citizenship may not be an issue, but as soon as a conflict arises, balancing competing loyalties becomes challenging.

In the business world, the Enron scandal was a case of divided loyalties, causing the collapse of one of the largest companies in the United States. The self-dealing of a few insiders was a classic example of disloyalty to the company and shareholders. That is why business and non-profit organizations are serious about conflicts of interest. Board members cannot benefit from deals made by the company or organization. Executives cannot manage competing businesses. Lawyers cannot represent both the plaintiff and the defendant. That is why you want a financial advisor who is a fiduciary, because he is required to have only your best interest in decisions and advice. That is why there are laws against insider trading in the stock market.

Competing loyalties is also a dilemma for people of faith. Muslims living in Western countries are caught between living according to the Koran and the laws of the country. It is easier to live in a predominately Muslim country where Sharia law syncs with religious beliefs. The same is true for Christians living in the Middle East. Inevitably, there will be conflicts of loyalty between God and country.

Loyalty has a hierarchy. My loyalty to my wife, for example, is going to supersede loyalty to my country, a baseball team, or even a friend. While we are instructed to obey the laws of our nation, there are times when loyalty to God trumps that command. Peter settled it by saying, "We must obey God rather than men" (Acts 5:29). If we are forced to choose between loyalty to God and loyalty to a person, God always wins.

There are also priorities of loyalty between people. While we are commanded to love everyone, it is impossible to be equally loyal. So when we are caught in the middle between two people we love, though awkward, those priorities already dictate which side of the fence we will end up on. We might get caught in the middle between two friends or two co-workers or two people who are married. Children of divorced parents can be torn between the two separated parents.

Loyalties generally fall into three categories: God, causes, and people, but the focus of this book is loyalty to people. So what do you do when you are pulled in two different directions? In this chapter we are going to look at the example of Jonathan.

As far as we know, the first time Jonathan met David was right after David killed Goliath. When David was summoned into the presence of King Saul to explain who he was, I Samuel 18:1 says, "The soul of Jonathan was knit to the soul of David, and Jonathan loved him as his own soul." That would have been fine except that his loyalty to his friend clashed with his loyalty and commitment to his father, the king. This also put David in an awkward situation of being loyal to both his friend and his king.

Theirs was not a casual friendship because Jonathan "made a covenant with David, because he loved him as his own soul" (1 Samuel 18:3). This was all-out commitment to the level that "Jonathan said to David, 'Whatever you say, I will do for you'" (1 Samuel 20:4).

As mentioned earlier, loyalty sometimes includes a written covenant or formal agreement. A marriage covenant states, "until death do us part." Other agreements are just understood, such as a company assuming you will be loyal if you enter an employment contract with them.

As a symbol of Jonathan's covenant, he "stripped himself of the robe that was on him and gave it to David, and his armor, and even his sword and his bow and his belt" (1 Samuel 18:4). That symbol of a commitment to loyalty is similar to the exchange of rings at a wedding.

This was all good until David started gaining popularity. "David went out and was successful wherever Saul sent him, so that Saul set him over the men of war. And this was good in the sight of all the people and also in the sight of Saul's servants" (1 Samuel 18:5). Saul's jealousy put Jonathan in the middle ground of discomfort and awkwardness. This put David in situations where he was dodging spears, living in caves, and running for his life. Jonathan approached his awkwardness in several ways.

Do Right

David may have had a loyal friend, but that relationship was complicated by his loyalty to Saul. Even though Saul was trying to kill him, David maintained a respect and commitment to the God-anointed king. "He said to his men, 'The LORD forbid that I should do this thing to my lord, the LORD's anointed, to put out my hand against him, seeing he is the LORD's anointed'" (1 Samuel 24:6). After passing up an opportunity to kill Saul in a cave, he told him, "Behold, this day your eyes have seen how the LORD gave you today into my hand in the cave. And some told me to kill you, but I spared you. I said, 'I will not put out my hand against my lord, for he is the LORD's anointed'" (1 Samuel 24:10).

Gene Edwards writes the following in his book, *The Tale of Three Kings:*

> David had a question: what do you do when someone throws a spear at you? Does it seem odd to you that David did not know the answer to this question? After all, everyone else in the world knows what to do when a spear is thrown at you. Why, you pick up the spear and throw it right back! "When someone throws a spear at you, David, just wrench it out of the wall and throw it back. Everyone else does, you can be sure." And in performing this small feat of returning thrown spears, you will prove many things: you are courageous. You stand for the right. You boldly stand against the wrong. You are tough and can't be pushed around. You will not stand for injustice or unfair treatment. You are the defender of the faith, keeper of the flame, detector of all heresy. You will not be wronged. All of these attributes then combine to prove that you are also a candidate for kingship. Yes, perhaps you are the Lord's anointed. After the order of king Saul. There is also a possibility that some twenty years after your coronation, you will be the most incredibly skilled spear thrower in all the realm. And also by then . . . Quite mad.[26]

Sometimes loyalty means taking the high road and not responding as we would like. It restrains our spear throwing. It means that we absorb the punch of someone's attack. Even

---

26 Gene Edwards, *A Tale of Three Kings,* Tyndale House Publishers, Carol Stream, 1980, p.23.

when they are unreasonable and turn against us, we do not retaliate.

Jonathan also had a dilemma. "And Saul spoke to Jonathan his son and to all his servants, that they should kill David. But Jonathan, Saul's son, delighted much in David. And Jonathan told David, 'Saul my father seeks to kill you'" (1 Samuel 19:1-2). How do you honor your father and your friend at the same time?

In this instance, the principle was rather simple. Loyalty does not mean blind loyalty. There is a higher authority in scripture that says do not kill [murder]. Therefore, Jonathan simply told David about the price on his head. His loyalty tipped toward his friend because he could not be loyal to someone who would demand disobedience. Ultimately, we are always to do right. Jonathan then took another approach to this dilemma.

Be a Mediator

Jonathan was not satisfied with being passive in this conflict. His loyalty to both Saul and David required that he do something.

And Jonathan spoke well of David to Saul his father and said to him, "Let not the king sin against his servant David, because he has not sinned against you, and because his deeds have brought good to you. For he took his life in his hand and he struck down the Philistine, and the LORD worked a great salvation for all Israel. You saw it, and rejoiced. Why then will you sin against innocent blood by killing David without cause?" And Saul listened to the voice of Jonathan. Saul swore, "As the LORD lives, he shall not be put to death." And Jonathan called David, and Jonathan reported to him all these things. And Jonathan brought David to Saul, and he was in his presence as before. (1 Samuel 19:4-7)

In this situation, mediation worked. Jonathan was able to restore the relationship. The advantage of being caught in the middle of conflict is that it positions you to facilitate a reconciliation like Jonathan did with his father and David. Sometimes it is easier to see both sides when you are in the middle. While Saul only saw one side, it was the role of Jonathan to help him see the other side. That may be the blessing of having relationships with two parties in a conflict.

There is a parallel story to this one where David's wife Michal also got caught in the middle between loyalty to her husband and loyalty to her father.

> Saul sent messengers to David's house to watch him, that he might kill him in the morning. But Michal, David's wife, told him, "If you do not escape with your life tonight, tomorrow you will be killed." So Michal let David down through the window, and he fled away and escaped. Michal took an image and laid it on the bed and put a pillow of goats' hair at its head and covered it with the clothes. And when Saul sent messengers to take David, she said, "He is sick." Then Saul sent the messengers to see David, saying, "Bring him up to me in the bed, that I may kill him." And when the messengers came in, behold, the image was in the bed, with the pillow of goats' hair at its head. Saul said to Michal, "Why have you deceived me thus and let my enemy go, so that he has escaped?" And Michal answered Saul, "He said to me, 'Let me go. Why should I kill you?'" (1 Samuel 19:11-17)

Michal was governed by the "do right" principle. She was not going to allow her father to kill her husband. The rest of the story, however, moves more into a gray area. She was willing to lie and deceive to be loyal to David. That action conflicts with the "do right" principle. This introduces that age-old question: is it ever right to do wrong in order to do right? Or to put it another way: is it acceptable to lie to save someone's life? Do the ends justify the means? The simple or perhaps simplistic answer is that there is not an escape clause to the Ten Commandments.

It takes wisdom to walk the fence between two who are at odds with each other, and you want to be loyal to both. The easiest approach would be to lie, but that is not acceptable. There are three other options: (1) tell all the truth (in other words, say everything you know), (2) withhold the truth (in other words don't volunteer information), (3) tell a half-truth (or rather, tell some of the truth but not all of it). The topic of situational ethics and ethical relativism is a multi-faceted discussion beyond the scope of this chapter, though Jesus indicated some laws are weightier than others: "Woe to you, scribes and Pharisees, hypocrites! For you tithe mint and dill and cumin, and have neglected the weightier matters of the law: justice and mercy and faithfulness" (Matthew 23:23).

Jonathan walked a fine line. He withheld information, but he did not outright lie like Michal did. Instead, he used his persuasive power to try to bring them together. Both Jonathan and Michal had David's best interest in mind, but Jonathan was able to do that without telling a lie. It takes wisdom to navigate through this scenario.

Do It with Candor

Jonathan found himself trying to keep a bully from beating up a friend. It can be dangerous to get caught in the middle since you might absorb a punch intended for the person you are protecting. This intervention strained Jonathan's relationship with his father.

We've already looked at Jonathan's straightforward, honest communication with his father to dissuade him from his animosity toward David. This time, his father listened to him and withdrew his death warrant. Unfortunately, this was a temporary truce, and David was again dodging spears. David connected with Jonathan again and asked,

"What have I done? What is my guilt? And what is my sin before your father, that he seeks my life?" And he said to him, "Far from it! You shall not die. Behold, my father does nothing either great or small without disclosing it to me. And why should my father hide this from me? It is not so." (1 Samuel 20:1-2)

Notice that Jonathan was forthright in explaining his relationship with his father. He didn't mince words or skirt around the issue. He sought to bring objectivity into the situation for David.

Jonathan spoke with candor as he told David, "If I knew that it was determined by my father that harm should come to you, would I not tell you?" (1 Samuel 20:9). That is candor. That is the outworking of loyalty when you are caught in the middle. It flows from the word *hesed* which we examined in chapter 7 about Ruth. David asked for that kind of response from Jonathan.

> "If I am still alive, show me the steadfast love [*hesed*] of the LORD, that I may not die; and do not cut off your steadfast love [*hesed*] from my house forever, when the LORD cuts off every one of the enemies of David from the face of the earth." And Jonathan made a covenant with the house of David, saying, "May the LORD take vengeance on David's enemies." And Jonathan made David swear again by his love for him, for he loved him as he loved his own soul. (1 Samuel 20:14-17)

Now the story gets a little murky. Jonathan and David concocted a plan to find out whether it was safe for David to come home. He was invited to a long feast with Saul but decided not to go. Instead, Jonathan needed to figure out Saul's demeanor toward David. When David didn't show up, Saul asked Jonathan why David was not there.

> Jonathan answered, "David earnestly asked leave of me to go to Bethlehem. He said, 'Let me go, for our clan holds a sacrifice in the city, and my brother has commanded me to be there. So now, if I have found favor in your eyes, let me get away and see my brothers.' For this reason he has not come to the king's table." (1 Samuel 20:28-29)

On the one hand, Jonathan was being loyal and protecting the next anointed king of Israel. On the other hand, he was deliberately either shading the truth or outright lying. We don't know if David really did go to Bethlehem, in which case this was not a lie.

Bethlehem was only 8.5 miles away, perhaps a three-hour walk, so it is entirely feasible David went there to meet with his clan. Giving the benefit of the doubt and assuming it was true, Jonathan was still withholding information. The question is whether that was wrong.

There is an interesting story when God told Samuel to go anoint David. "And Samuel said, 'How can I go? If Saul hears it, he will kill me.'" Notice that God said, "Take a heifer with you and say, 'I have come to sacrifice to the LORD'" (1 Samuel 16:2). We might conclude that God is condoning withholding truth or at least giving an alternative legitimate reason for going to anoint David.

Whether Jonathan was right or wrong in what he did, it points out the dilemma that you will experience when you are trying to be loyal to two people at the same time. It is going to take great wisdom and character to do right. It will never be easy.

A couple of things happened because of this plan. Saul's rage revealed he was still out to kill David.

> Then Saul's anger was kindled against Jonathan, and he said to him, "You son of a perverse, rebellious woman, do I not know that you have chosen the son of Jesse to your own shame, and to the shame of your mother's nakedness? For as long as the son of Jesse lives on the earth, neither you nor your kingdom shall be established. Therefore send and bring him to me, for he shall surely die." (1 Samuel 20:30-31)

Second, Jonathan's life was in danger as his own father hurled a spear at him. Perhaps the main lesson here is that it may not be possible to be loyal to both parties in conflict. Ultimately, Jonathan lost his relationship with his father. This is an unfortunate facet of the topic of loyalty. We live in a fallen world with fallen people, and sometimes things just can't be fixed. Thirty-six percent of those who responded to my survey said their experience with disloyalty was never resolved. We may have to accept that sometimes it is a no-win situation, and we have to live with unresolved circumstances. That is a painful realization.

The Rest of the Story

Managing your thoughts and feelings about people who betray you is a challenge. A test for how you are doing with this is how you respond when something bad happens to them. Your natural inclination will be to secretly think they deserve it and have it coming to them. If, however, you have truly forgiven, you will respond like David.

Upon hearing of Saul's death,

> Then David took hold of his clothes and tore them, and so did all the men who were with him. And they mourned and wept and fasted until evening for Saul and for Jonathan his son and for the people of the Lord and for the house of Israel, because they had fallen by the sword. (2 Samuel 1:11-12)

Additionally he said, "Daughters of Israel, weep over Saul" (2 Samuel 1:24).

You can also read about David's lament for his friend Jonathan in 2 Samuel 1. It is a poem recorded in the book of Jashur and memorized by the people of Israel. This highlights the importance and value of loyalty. This lament ends by David saying:

> I am distressed for you, my brother Jonathan;
> very pleasant have you been to me;
> your love to me was extraordinary,
> surpassing the love of women.
> How the mighty have fallen,
> and the weapons of war perished! (2 Samuel 1:26-27)

David never got over it and did not forget his commitment to his friend. "And David said, 'Is there still anyone left of the house of Saul, that I may show him kindness for Jonathan's sake?'" (2 Samuel 9:1). They located Jonathan's son so David could restore property to his family, and "Mephibosheth lived in Jerusalem, for he ate always at the king's table" (2 Samuel 9:13).

We could all wish for loyal friends like Jonathan. At the end of his life, David valued the loyalty he had experienced and wanted that more than anything else for his son. King David prayed the following: "Grant to Solomon my son a whole heart that he may keep your commandments, your testimonies, and your statutes, performing all, and that he may build the palace for which I have made provision" (1 Chronicles 29:19 NKJV).

Unfortunately, God did not answer David's prayer in the affirmative. We read that "when Solomon was old his wives turned away his heart after other gods, and his heart was not wholly true to the LORD his God, as was the heart of David his father" (1 Kings 11:4). Sad.

A pastor friend who experienced disloyalty in his ministry wrote the following:

Yes, to say that I/we were stabbed in the back would be an understatement of some magnitude. But the Lord graciously sustained us and taught us much . . . a lot I needed to learn. Psalm 73 became my favorite psalm through that time.

Many of the Psalms emerged from difficult circumstances, and this is one that you might want to put on your reading list when you are going through the valley of disloyalty.

Psalm 73
A Psalm of Asaph

Truly God is good to Israel,
to those who are pure in heart.
2 But as for me, my feet had almost stumbled,
my steps had nearly slipped.
3 For I was envious of the arrogant
when I saw the prosperity of the wicked.
4 For they have no pangs until death;
their bodies are fat and sleek.
5 They are not in trouble as others are;
they are not stricken like the rest of mankind.

⁶ Therefore pride is their necklace;
violence covers them as a garment.
⁷ Their eyes swell out through fatness;
their hearts overflow with follies.
⁸ They scoff and speak with malice;
loftily they threaten oppression.
⁹ They set their mouths against the heavens,
and their tongue struts through the earth.
¹⁰ Therefore his people turn back to them,
and find no fault in them.
¹¹ And they say, "How can God know?
Is there knowledge in the Most High?"
¹² Behold, these are the wicked;
always at ease, they increase in riches.
¹³ All in vain have I kept my heart clean
and washed my hands in innocence.
¹⁴ For all the day long I have been stricken
and rebuked every morning.
¹⁵ If I had said, "I will speak thus,"
I would have betrayed the generation of your children.
¹⁶ But when I thought how to understand this,
it seemed to me a wearisome task,
¹⁷ until I went into the sanctuary of God;
then I discerned their end.
¹⁸ Truly you set them in slippery places;
you make them fall to ruin.
¹⁹ How they are destroyed in a moment,
swept away utterly by terrors!
²⁰ Like a dream when one awakes,
O Lord, when you rouse yourself, you despise them as
phantoms.
²¹ When my soul was embittered,
when I was pricked in heart,
²² I was brutish and ignorant;
I was like a beast toward you.
²³ Nevertheless, I am continually with you;
you hold my right hand.

²⁴ You guide me with your counsel,
and afterward you will receive me to glory.
²⁵ Whom have I in heaven but you?
And there is nothing on earth that I desire besides you.
²⁶ My flesh and my heart may fail,
but God is the strength of my heart and my portion forever.
²⁷ For behold, those who are far from you shall perish;
you put an end to everyone who is unfaithful to you.
²⁸ But for me it is good to be near God;
I have made the Lord GOD my refuge,
that I may tell of all your works.

11

URIAH

When loyalty costs

Uriah is an example of dedication and commitment to a person, a team, and a cause, but loyalty cost Uriah his life. Though his is an extreme example, we need to know that loyalty sometimes has its price. We may be remembered as either a traitor or a loyal friend. We can decide which one.

You probably know the story well, but to set the stage, here is a review. It was springtime, the season when kings went to war, but this time David sent Joab to lead the armies of Israel while he stayed home. The city of David was terraced, so it would have been easy to look down on homes below. From his housetop it was possible for him to see Bathsheba bathing, and he summoned her for an adulterous affair.

Bathsheba became pregnant, so David devised a plan to cover his sin. Calling Uriah back from the battle, David made it feasible for him to go home to his wife so that the child would be assumed to be his. Uriah, however, refused to indulge in the comforts of home while his colleagues were on the battlefront and thereby foiled David's efforts to cover his tracks.

Plan B for David was to have Uriah sent to the battlefront where he would most certainly be killed. Rabbah, the city they were attacking, was located right in the middle of what today is Amman, the capital of Jordan. The ruins are still there. The Citadel is on the highest hill in the city called Jebel al Qala. The town of Rabbah was perched on the top of a dome, so there was no easy way to attack. From any direction, soldiers would have to climb straight up, making them easy targets from the top. There was no way for Uriah to survive.

When David received news of Uriah's death, he commented in an amazingly cavalier and calloused way: "Do not let this matter displease you, for the sword devours now one and now another" (2 Samuel 11:25). Uriah lost his life on that hillside, all because of his loyalty.

The Purpose of Loyalty

Uriah was a foreigner. According to Genesis 10:15, the Hittites were the descendants of Canaan who lived in part of the promised land. Their religion was one of nature worship of various gods of the earth, sky and weather. This was a pagan nation that God had commanded Israel to drive out of the land (Exodus 23:28-33).

The Hittites would have been considered enemies, but it appears that Uriah shifted his allegiance to Israel and joined their army. Since his name means "Yahweh is my light," it is reasonable to assume he converted to follow the God of Israel. Uriah gives us a window into the purpose of God for the nation of Israel. The descendants of Abraham were meant to be a light to the world for the declaration of the grace of God. They often forgot that and wallowed in their own self-importance, thinking that as God's chosen people they were the sole reason for their own existence. From the very beginning, God told Abraham "in you all the families of the earth shall be blessed" (Genesis 12:3). They often forgot the word *all* and assumed it was just their families that would be blessed.

And the scripture, foreseeing that God would justify the heathen through faith, preached before the gospel unto Abraham, saying, In thee shall all nations be blessed. So then they which be of faith are blessed with faithful Abraham. (Galatians 3:8-9)

Uriah was an illustration of God's intent for Gentiles to come to faith. This concept was reiterated to the nation of Israel over and over throughout the Old Testament.

Israel is to be "a light for the nations." (Isaiah 42:6)

I will make you as a light for the nations, that my salvation may reach to the end of the earth. (Isaiah 49:6)

But for this purpose I have raised you up, to show you my power, so that my name may be proclaimed in all the earth. (Exodus 9:16)

You shall be my treasured possession among all peoples, for all the earth is mine; and you shall be to me a kingdom of priests and a holy nation. (Exodus 9:5-6)

You shall treat the stranger who sojourns with you as the native among you, and you shall love him as yourself, for you were strangers in the land of Egypt: I am the LORD your God. (Leviticus 19:34)

So that all the peoples of the earth may know that the hand of the LORD is mighty. (Joshua 4:24)

Likewise, when a foreigner, who is not of your people Israel, comes from a far country for your name's sake . . . in order that all the peoples of the earth may know your name and fear you. (I Kings 8:41-43)

Declare his glory among the nations, his marvelous works among all the peoples! (1 Chronicles 16:24)

All the ends of the earth shall remember and turn to the LORD, and all the families of the nations shall worship before you. (Psalm 22:27)

Let all the earth fear the LORD; let all the inhabitants of the world stand in awe of him! (Psalm 33:8)

All the nations you have made shall come and worship before you, O LORD, and shall glorify your name. (Psalm 86:9)

Praise the LORD, all nations! Extol him, all peoples! (Psalm 117:1)

And they shall declare my glory among the nations. (Isaiah 66:19)

For my temple will be known as a temple where all nations may pray. (Isaiah 56:7)

I will set my justice for a light to the peoples [Gentiles]. (Isaiah 51:4)

For from the rising of the sun to its setting my name will be great among the nations. (Malachi 1:11)

Israel was to be a missionary nation, and it appeared to have worked with Uriah. By leaving the Hittites and joining the Israelites, he would probably have faced prejudice, racism, and rejection as he established himself in his newly adopted nation. We get a hint of what Jewish people thought about Hittites from Rebecca's comments to her son Isaac: "I loathe my life because of the Hittite women. If Jacob marries one of the Hittite women like these, one of the women of the land, what good will my life be to me?" (Genesis 27:46). Uriah may have always been considered an outsider and interloper, but despite this, he developed an extreme loyalty to his adopted country and king.

The Relationships of Loyalty

Uriah was one of David's mighty men. In 1 Chronicles 11:10 we read, "Now these are the chiefs of David's mighty men, who gave him strong support in his kingdom, together with all Israel, to make him king, according to the word of the LORD concerning Israel." These were the elite warriors of Israel, perhaps similar to Special Forces like Navy Seals and Army Rangers. These would be the best of the best and certainly some of the most trusted as they helped David to establish his kingdom. As a foreigner, Uriah had risen to heights of leadership and credibility in the Israelite army.

Whereas current day leaders rarely go to the battlefront, back in these days the kings would go out to war. It would be reasonable to think that David had fought side by side with Uriah. While David could not possibly know the names of thousands of warriors, he most certainly would have personally known the thirty-seven elite soldiers who fought with him (2 Samuel 23:39).

My survey indicated that over half of disloyalty situations happened with people who were in a close working relationship and roughly the same percentage had a close personal relationship. In this instance, Uriah's loyalty was rewarded with disloyalty, and to make things even worse, he was a team member and possibly a close acquaintance.

It is incongruous that David could have acted toward Uriah like he did, but it forewarns us that anything is possible. Even the best relationships can fall apart. Sometimes loyalty only flows one way.

The Impact of Disloyalty

Uriah's life was intertwined with other key leaders through marriage. His wife, Bathsheba, was the granddaughter of Ahithophel, one of David's key advisors. Bathsheba's father was Eliam who was also one of David's mighty men, so those two would have been in battle together. All these people knew each other or were related. In addition to Uriah losing his wife and his life, an additional casualty was the relationship Ahithophel had with David. He walked away from his position of leadership with David and joined Absalom in his rebellion as a way to punish David for his adultery and murder.

The collateral damage of David's sin spread wide. In addition to impacting Uriah, Eliam, Ahithophel, and other family members, David's sin resulted in the death of his baby, and the wreckage continued for generations. Through Nathan, God said to David:

> You have struck down Uriah the Hittite with the sword and have taken his wife to be your wife and have killed him with the sword of the Ammonites. Now therefore the sword shall never depart from your house, because you have despised me and have taken the wife of Uriah the Hittite to be your wife . . . I will raise up evil against you out of your own house. And I will take your wives before your eyes and give them to your neighbor, and he shall lie with your wives in the sight of this sun. For you did it secretly, but I will do this thing before all Israel and before the sun . . . by this deed you have utterly scorned the LORD, the child who is born to you shall die. (2 Samuel 12:9-12, 14)

Murdering Uriah did not solve David's problems. After the time for mourning ended, David took Bathsheba to be his wife. "But the thing that David had done displeased the LORD" (2 Samuel 11:27). God sent the prophet Nathan to confront David regarding his sin. Nathan told a story of a rich man with many sheep and cattle and a poor man who had only one ewe lamb that was like a daughter to him. The rich man refused to use a sheep of his own to prepare a meal for a traveler and instead took the poor man's ewe. "David's anger was greatly kindled against the man" and even said the man should die and must pay four times the amount the lamb was worth (2 Samuel 12:5–6). "Then Nathan said to David, 'You are the man!'" (2 Samuel 12:7).

The Impact of Loyalty

Uriah was remarkably loyal to his comrades on the battle-front. When offered an opportunity to sleep in his own bed, he said,

> The ark and Israel and Judah dwell in booths, and my lord Joab and the servants of my lord are camping in the open field. Shall I then go to my house, to eat and to drink and to lie with my wife? As you live, and as your soul lives, I will not do this thing. (2 Samuel 11:11)

His loyalty to his band of brothers prioritized his decisions. It was inconceivable to him that he could be in the comfort of his own home while his fellow warriors were at the battlefront.

Uriah was so faithful that he personally delivered his own death warrant. David wrote a letter to Joab and sent it by the hand of Uriah. In the letter he wrote, "Set Uriah in the forefront of the hardest fighting, and then draw back from him, that he may be struck down, and die" (2 Samuel 11:15). He was unaware during the forty-five-mile journey from Jerusalem to the battle-front that the message he safely guarded was his death sentence. His faithfulness took him up the hill toward Rabbah to be first in line to face the onslaught of the enemy above him.

Things don't always turn out well when you are loyal; in fact, your loyalty may indeed be the catalyst for trouble in your life. Uriah did nothing wrong to deserve this treatment.

Some make the false promise that if you follow God, you will be prosperous. Jesus told us that in this world we will have trouble (John 16:33). So the lesson here is that our loyalty is for the benefit of others, not our own. That is the essence of love. It is the definition of *hesed*. It is an application of Jesus' observation that "Greater love has no one than this, that someone lay down his life for his friends" (John 15:13).

Loyalty is a commitment to stay together through both good and bad times. The tough times are painful because walking beside another means you, too, might suffer. Loyalty to a company could result in a pay cut if business goes bad. Loyalty to a spouse means you stay beside them "in sickness and in health." Loyalty to a friend may mean suffering loss alongside of them. The most painful of all is when you are loyal to someone, and he or she walks away from you. It can be costly to be loyal.

What a tragic story! Uriah establishes a standard for amazing loyalty but illustrates the high price that must sometimes be paid. Yet we learn that God takes our messes and still produces good things out of it. In an astounding sample of His grace, the Lord took the next baby from Solomon and Bathsheba and produced Solomon, one of the wisest and greatest kings of the Jewish nation. Out of that same lineage came Jesus who is the Savior of the world. Also out of this heartbreak, we have passages of scripture like Psalm 51.

> Have mercy on me, O God,
>   according to your steadfast love;
>   according to your abundant mercy
>   blot out my transgressions.
> Wash me thoroughly from my iniquity,
>   and cleanse me from my sin!
> For I know my transgressions,
>   and my sin is ever before me.
> Against you, you only, have I sinned
>   and done what is evil in your sight,
>   so that you may be justified in your words
>   and blameless in your judgment.
> Behold, I was brought forth in iniquity,
>   and in sin did my mother conceive me.
> Behold, you delight in truth in the inward being,
>   and you teach me wisdom in the secret heart.

Purge me with hyssop, and I shall be clean;
    wash me, and I shall be whiter than snow.
Let me hear joy and gladness;
    let the bones that you have broken rejoice.
Hide your face from my sins,
    and blot out all my iniquities.
Create in me a clean heart, O God,
    and renew a right spirit within me.
Cast me not away from your presence,
    and take not your Holy Spirit from me.
Restore to me the joy of your salvation,
    and uphold me with a willing spirit.
Then I will teach transgressors your ways,
    and sinners will return to you.
Deliver me from blood guiltiness, O God,
    O God of my salvation,
    and my tongue will sing aloud of your righteous-
        ness.
O LORD, open my lips,
    and my mouth will declare your praise.
For you will not delight in sacrifice, or I would give it;
    you will not be pleased with a burnt offering.
The sacrifices of God are a broken spirit;
    a broken and contrite heart, O God, you will not
        despise.
Do good to Zion in your good pleasure;
    build up the walls of Jerusalem;
then will you delight in right sacrifices,
    in burnt offerings and whole burnt offerings;
    then bulls will be offered on your altar.

12

DOING SOMETHING

Marcus Aurelius was considered one of the greatest Roman emperors. He ruled from A.D. 161 to 180. One of the amazing things about him was his response to those who were disloyal. From the "Daily Stoic" we read the following story:

Late in his reign, sick and possibly near death, Stoic Emperor Marcus Aurelius received surprising news. His old friend and most trusted general, Avidius Cassius, had rebelled in Syria. Having heard the emperor was vulnerable or possibly dead, the ambitious general declared himself Caesar and assumed the throne.

Marcus should have been angry. After all, this man was trying to take his job and possibly his life. If we think about what other emperors did to their rivals and enemies, for instance Nero killed his own mother and Otho had Galba murdered in 69 A.D. and paraded his head around Rome, it makes Marcus's response all the more unusual. Because he didn't immediately set out to crush this man who had betrayed him, who threatened his life, his family, and his legacy. Instead, Marcus did nothing. He even kept the news secret from his troops, who might have been enraged or provoked on his behalf—and simply waited: Would Cassius come to his senses?

The man did not. And so Marcus Aurelius called a council of his soldiers and made a rather extraordinary announcement. They would march against Cassius and obtain the "great prize of war and of victory." But of course, because it was Marcus, this war prize was something wholly different.

Marcus informed them of his plan to capture Cassius, but not kill him. Instead, he would " . . . forgive a man who has wronged one, to remain a friend to one who has transgressed friendship, to continue faithful to one who has broken faith."

In a true Stoic fashion, Marcus had controlled his perceptions. He wasn't angry, he didn't despise his enemy. He would not say an ill word against him. He would not take it personally. Then he acted—rightly and firmly—ordering troops to Rome to calm the panicking crowds and then set out to do what must be done: protect the empire, put down a threat.

As he told his men, if there was one profit they could derive from this awful situation that they had not wanted, it would be to "settle this affair well and show to all mankind that there is a right way to deal even with civil wars."

Of course, as so often happens, even the most well-intentioned plans can be interrupted by others. For both Cassius and Marcus, their destiny was changed when a lone assassin struck Cassius down in Egypt, three months later. His dream of empire ended right there. Marcus's initial hope to be able to forgive, in person, his betrayer ended as well.

Arriving in the provinces shortly after the death of Cassius, Marcus refused to put any co-conspirators to death. He declined to prosecute any of the senators or governors who had endorsed or expressed support for the uprising. And when other senators insisted on death sentences for their peers associated with the rebellion, he wrote them simply: "I implore you, the senate, to keep my reign unstained by the blood of any senator. May it never happen." Marcus chose to forgive essentially everyone involved. He wouldn't take any of it personally. He'd be a better person, a better leader for it.[27]

If a non-Christian Roman emperor could act in such a way, surely believers can. The character and actions of a pagan emperor should not exceed those of a Spirit-filled believer, yet to our shame we often fail to respond to disloyalty in the right way. As we wrap up this book on loyalty and disloyalty, my encouragement is to do something practical with what you have read. This is the focus of this last chapter.

Seek Peace Aggressively

Romans 12:18 is a fascinating verse. "If possible, so far as it depends on you, live peaceably with all." The last part of the verse (that we should live at peace with others) is obviously what a Christian should do, but it is the phrase "if possible" that captures my attention. This is a first-class condition in Greek, a simple statement followed by an imperative. We are commanded to live peaceably but, being realistic, that may not always be possible.

The point is we are instructed to be proactive in seeking peace even though it may not happen. One of the disappointing things in my survey is that most times where there was disloyalty, there was a delay of or no resolution.

Since disloyalty involves two people, it takes two people to reconcile. One person can forgive without being asked to forgive, but reconciliation involves both parties, so that is what may be

27 https://dailystoic.com/stoic-response-betrayal/

implied in this verse. It is more than that, however, since there is an admonishment to be aggressive in trying to bring resolution. It is a command.

That is the intention of Matthew 18 where the offended party has the responsibility of approaching the offender. We do not have the luxury of sitting back and waiting for someone else to approach us. We cannot control how others respond, but we can control whether we are seeking to reconcile.

The verse preceding Romans 12:17 says: "Repay no one evil for evil." Our natural response is to retaliate, to wish bad on those who have stabbed us in the back, but the context here commands us to reject retribution. Instead, multiple verses command us to live at peace with others.

> Salt is good, but if the salt has lost its saltiness, how will you make it salty again? Have salt in yourselves, and be at peace with one another. (Mark 9:50)

> Finally, brothers, rejoice. Aim for restoration, comfort one another, agree with one another, live in peace; and the God of love and peace will be with you. (2 Corinthians 13:11)

> Be at peace among yourselves. (I Thessalonians 5:13)

> Blessed are the peacemakers, for they shall be called sons of God. (Matthew 5:9)

> Strive for peace with everyone. (Hebrews 12:14)

> But love your enemies, and do good, and lend, expecting nothing in return, and your reward will be great, and you will be sons of the Most High, for he is kind to the ungrateful and the evil. Be merciful, even as your Father is merciful. (Luke 6:35-36)

The words in Romans 12:20-21 come from Proverbs 25:21-22: "If your enemy is hungry, feed him; if he is thirsty, give him something to drink; for by so doing you will heap burning coals on his head. Do not be overcome by evil, but overcome evil with good." It is incongruous on a human level to do good to those who treat us badly, yet Jesus taught us to turn the other cheek (Matthew 5:39) and to love our enemies (Matthew 5:43-48). Jesus modeled it to us: "When he was reviled, he did not revile in return; when he suffered, he did not threaten, but continued entrusting himself to him who judges justly" (1 Peter 2:23).

In His Sermon on the Mount, Jesus preached, "Blessed are the peacemakers." These people are proactive in restoring peace between people. They are intentional. One of the cravings of a human soul is to have peace, but it takes work to achieve it.

The Apostle Paul used this concept of *peacemaker* in other places. "For in him all the fullness of God was pleased to dwell, and through him to reconcile to himself all things, whether on earth or in heaven, making peace by the blood of his cross" (Colossians 1:19-20). Ironically, believers enjoy the peace that comes through the brutal killing of Jesus, yet we won't work for it between ourselves. Our default ought to be to seek peace. Disloyalty should be the last thing on our agenda, but when it happens, we are to immediately seek reconciliation.

Most of us don't like conflict. We tend to flee from it or try to ignore it. We certainly don't want to go head-to-head in trying to resolve it, but we don't really have an option if we are going to comply with Romans 12:18. Even if unsuccessful, we still have a responsibility to be civil and treat our enemies with kindness. Our strategy should never be retaliation by trying to overcome evil with evil.

But I say to you who hear, Love your enemies, do good to those who hate you, bless those who curse you, pray for those who abuse you. To one who strikes you on the cheek, offer the other also, and from one who takes away your cloak do not withhold your tunic either. Give to everyone who begs from you, and from one who takes away your goods do not demand them back. And as you wish that others would do to you, do so to them. (Luke 6:27-31)

Even men like Spurgeon struggled with this issue. With a twist of cynicism, he said,

> Some people will quarrel, and it is barely possible to keep upon good terms with them. In their case we must do our best, and if after all, we cannot live peaceably with them, it will be fortunate for us if we can move off and live without them.[28]

I mentioned to a counselor who specializes in conflict resolution that there must be something wrong with him to want to do that kind of work. He pointed out that, first of all, it is just the right thing to do, but then he also said it is such a sweet victory when reconciliation does take place. The floodgates of blessing burst on us as we enjoy both peace and an enhanced relationship with the other person. While we might end up framing an unresolved conflict as "irreconcilable differences," we should not be happy with that standoff. Most certainly we cannot hold on to resentment or seek to retaliate. The bonus of peacemaking is that we have peace.

Application

A legitimate question after every sermon or Bible study is "so what?" We don't want to just acquire knowledge; we need to apply it. It would be a waste of time for you to read this book and not do anything with it. Here are some practical steps to take.

Inventory loyalty in your life.
- Make a list of people you could be loyal to.
- Make a list of institutions/organizations you should be loyal to.
- Make a list of causes you could be loyal to.

---

28 Charles Spurgeon, *Morning and Evening,* November 17, Crossway, 2003.

- Give yourself a grade for how you are doing with each of these groups.
- Write down action steps to improve or maintain your loyalty with all of these.

Inventory disloyalty in your life.
- What disloyal person came to mind when you read this book?
- Can you think of anyone to whom you have been disloyal?
- Was relationship resolved to the point where you can look the person in the eye and be at peace?
- If it was never resolved, when will you be proactive in approaching the person to seek reconciliation?
- Have you truly forgiven the other individual regardless of whether he or she asked for forgiveness?
- Are you demonstrating grace and kindness to the other person?
- Is there residual bitterness because of past disloyalty? (Ephesians 4:31)

Eleazar

We have briefly examined ten illustrations of loyalty and disloyalty, but let me close with one last story. It is found in 2 Samuel 23:9-10.

And next to him among the three mighty men was Eleazar the son of Dodo, son of Ahohi. He was with David when they defied the Philistines who were gathered there for battle, and the men of Israel withdrew. He rose and struck down the Philistines until his hand was weary, and his hand clung to the sword. And the LORD brought about a great victory that day, and the people returned after him only to spoil.

The setting of this passage is a discussion of thirty men who were exceptional warriors with King David who fought battles against the Philistines. Of these thirty there were three "mighty men," including Eleazar. Notice several things about the topic of loyalty from these two verses.

We are told, "The men of Israel withdrew." Someone had sounded retreat, and everyone except David and Eleazar fled. What a vivid picture of loyalty! David was under attack and not about to turn and run, so Eleazar stayed with him. That is exactly what loyalty demands. When a friend is left alone in the battlefield of life, the loyal person stays with him.

We are also told that "He rose and struck down the Philistines until his hand was weary, and his hand clung to the sword." Eleazar faithfully stayed with David till his hand cramped, and he could not uncurl his fingers from the handle. Together they won the battle. The tenacity of this mighty warrior is an example of radical commitment. We want people who will stay with us for the duration and last until they are exhausted.

The following statement is exasperating: "And the people returned after him only to spoil." What gall! Eleazar was loyal, yet the disloyal reaped the benefits. But this points to the very heart of loyalty. We do it not because of what we can get out of it, but rather because it is right. We've already seen that loyalty will cost us something. In Eleazar's instance it not only meant physical pain and exhaustion but also the frustration of watching hyena-like scavengers take advantage of his work.

When we look up the word *loyal* in the dictionary, there should be a picture of Eleazar. I'm left with the question of whether I am being Eleazar-like in the life of someone else.

But Wait—There's More!

And now a final word from my little sister who said, "Paul, you need to tell your readers how to work through the pain of betrayal." So thank you, Karen, for helping with this chapter. She has her master's in Christian counseling and has been an inner healing prayer minister since 2001.

126

Disloyalty hurts because it attacks the core of our being. Knowing it might happen doesn't necessarily soften the blow when it does. We know how we should respond, but what if we fall short? Here's a simple exercise to try.

Paul used the visual of a sword in your back, but your betrayer's words might look more like poison-tipped arrows aimed at your heart or like someone turning his back on you and walking away, leaving you doubled over with a stomach punch. You may even see yourself as a rug that someone stepped on with muddy boots.

Begin with your own visual of disloyalty; then sit quietly before the Lord as you feel the pain and invite Him into your picture. Some clients report how Jesus Himself becomes a shield of protection, absorbing the blow or the arrows. Or He lifts them to a standing position and washes off the mud with Living Water. Watch in your visual how He heals the wounds in your body, removing the poison, applying salve, or regrafting the skin. And listen for His sweet words of truth.

If you try this exercise and nothing changes, you can be sure there is a protective part of your heart that is standing in the way of your healing. As my brother Paul said, most of us have a knee-jerk reaction to disloyalty, attempting to protect our hearts through our own efforts. Blame is a shifting of pain. As long as we focus on what the other person did or did not do, we won't have to face what we're feeling inside. God is a gentleman, and He will never violate our will. Harboring anger, running from or denying the pain, seeking retaliation, hiding, going numb, making vows, holding onto unforgiveness, or building walls can all prevent us from hearing God's truth.

This guardian behavior may be a quick-fix solution of choice, but holding onto it for too long can turn toxic. Anger is a great protection from feeling hurt, but after a while, it will consume you like a forest fire. Unhealed wounds turn gangrenous with bitterness. A vow like "I'll never let anyone hurt me again" runs a stake in the ground and chains you to isolation.

Christians love to urge forgiveness as a first step in the healing process, and so we grit our teeth and choose to forgive

. . . over and over, but it may not stick if there is unresolved pain. Unforgiveness is like a rope tying you to the person who wronged you. To become free, you must unhook the rope from your belt loop. It doesn't mean what the person did was acceptable; it simply means you release him from the debt he owes you.

Ask the Lord to show you what your protection looks like. Is it a black cloud? A person with a sword of retaliation? A shield? An ice cube? A red-hot fire? A wall? A fist in the air? A pointed finger (blaming another for your pain)? What are you doing that you need to stop? Do you need to lower your finger or fist and feel the pain? Lay down your shield and feel naked and vulnerable? Are you willing for God to douse the flames of your anger and feel the fear underneath? Incidentally, if any part of your visual contains black or looks like a tornado or whirlwind, simply say to the black demonic entity, "The Lord rebuke you," and watch what happens!

If your heart is unwilling to feel the pain under the protective behavior, ask yourself why. There's usually a lie holding it in place. Ask the Lord to show you the truth. Again, He will never force you to relinquish your anger, your wall of protection, or your sword. You get to choose.

Perhaps this incident of disloyalty taps into a similar pain in your past. That's why it's called a trigger. As you sit with your present pain, what memory comes to the surface? If your heart is willing to go back to that memory and feel the pain in it, ask the Lord for truth to replace the lies that hold the pain in place. Working through the memory till it becomes peaceful will often release the pain in the present circumstances.

Sometimes sitting quietly before the Lord and releasing to Him what you are feeling is all it takes to move on. You recognize the other person acted out of his or her own pain, and their behavior was their own pain management. But when the wounds are deep, it might take a loyal friend or counselor to walk you through the process. There is no shame in asking for help.

Healing is an experience between you and God. Reconciliation is between two people. You cannot force another person to heal, and neither can you force reconciliation. One client described her attempt at reconciliation this way: I am on one side of a deep canyon, and the other person is on the other bank. We used to have a solid bridge of friendship between us, but she chopped up her side of the bridge. I keep throwing her a rope ladder, but she refuses to grab it. I feel lost and hurt.

I handed the client a box of crayons and a blank sheet of paper and asked her to draw what her hurt looked like. She sketched a gaping hole in her torso with blood dripping to the floor.

After she invited the Lord into the picture and He healed the wound, she asked Him what to do about the rope ladder. He said, "You have a choice: keep looking at your former friend or turn around and see all the people who want relationship with you."

"But I'm too loyal to abandon her," she said. "I'll never walk away."

"If she wants to, she can request the bridge again," He said. "She gets to decide."

The next day, astonished, she read this meme on Facebook: "Learning how to leave people alone and moving on with your life is a needed skill. You must master it."

An attempt at reconciliation is best expedited after you come to complete inner peace. Writing letters or emails or confronting in person while triggered only stirs the pot and creates more chaos. This I know from personal experience.

And, finally, a word about inordinate loyalty. If you find yourself caught in the trap of following a controlling leader, start by identifying your emotions and beliefs. Perhaps you feel fear. Maybe you're afraid of losing your job, losing friends, or losing face. Maybe it's tied into your self-worth when you're around powerful people. Ask, "How would it feel if I quit following him?" Or "What need is this person satisfying that should be fulfilled by God alone?" Perhaps you're the leader who's been accused of being a controller. There's always emotion behind that behavior. Are you willing to face what you're feeling and ask the Lord for help? Humility will go a long way toward mending broken fences.

Karen (Seger) Keegan
MKMinistry.org

ADDENDUM

Results of the Loyalty/Disloyalty Survey

I am responding as a	Ministry Leader	Business Leader
	93.1%	6.9%

Age	
20-29	.92%
30-39	13.85%
40-49	16.62%
50-59	21.23
60-69	30.46
70+	16.92

Sex	Female 9%	Male 91 %

Have you ever experienced someone being disloyal to you as a leader?	Yes	No
	84.7%	15.3%

With the one example of disloyalty you are thinking of, check as many of the boxes below that you feel would characterize the type of disloyalty you have experienced.	
Public criticism of your character (lack of spiritual walk or godly characteristics)	10.5%
Public criticism of your capacity (lack of ability in an area)	10.9%
Public criticism of your position on doctrine	6.2%
Public criticism of your social/political stance	3.3%
Public criticism of your interpersonal skills (lack of empathy, care, sarcasm, cynicism, too task-oriented)	6.8%
Public criticism of your work product (speeches, events, writings)	5.1%

Gossip to undercut your credibility, challenge your position	16.4%
Outright lies or slander to destroy your reputation	12.1%
Making, participating in, organizational moves to minimize or eliminate your role	10%
Refusing to support you when you made organizational changes	10.5%
Refusing to support you when others challenged your role	8.2%
Other	

Regarding this significant disloyalty event in your life, approximately how long would you say it lasted before it was resolved?	
One Day	1%
One Week	2%
One Month	14.6%
One Year	18.8%
Over One Year	27.9%
It has not been resolved	35.7%

On a scale of 1-5, how severely did disloyalty impact your ministry/work (1=low, 5=high)	
1	.35%
2	20.3%
3	22.6%
4	23.9%
5	23.9%

On a scale of 1-5, how severely did disloyalty impact you personally (1=low, 5=high)	
1	4.7%
2	8.6%
3	20.5%
4	30.3%
5	35.7%

On a scale of 1-5, if someone was disloyal to you, would you characterize him or her as someone who was in a close work/ministry relationship with you or a distant work/ministry relationship (1 = close and 5 = distant)	
1	45.5%
2	22.4%
3	15.6%
4	11.4%
5	5.2%

On a scale of 1-5, if someone was disloyal to you, would you characterize him or her as someone who was in close personal relationship with you or distant personal relationship (1 = close and 5 = distant)	
1	24.6%
2	21.4%
3	25.6%
4	20.1%
5	8.4%

Finally, on a related issue, have you ever been a part of an organization where unhealthy loyalty (not being allowed to question the leader, i.e., "worshipping" the leader, etc.) was practiced?	Yes	No
	57.2%	42.8%

Made in the USA
Columbia, SC
24 July 2023

20778183R00080